The Poetry of Adelaide Anne Proctor

Volume II

Adelaide Anne Procter was born on 30th October, 1825 at 25 Bedford Square in the Bloomsbury district of London. Her literary career began whilst still a teenager. Many of her poems were published by the great Charles Dickens in his periodicals Household Words and All the Year Round before being later published in book form.

A voracious reader, Procter was largely self-taught, though she did study at Queen's College in Harley Street in 1850. Her interest in poetry grew from an early age.

Procter published her first poem, Ministering Angels, while still a teenager in 1843.

By 1853 she was submitting pieces to Dickens's Household Words under her pseudonym Mary Berwick, electing that this way her work would be judged for its own worth rather than on the friendship between her father and Dickens. Dickens didn't learn of her true identity for over a year.

Minstering Angels was to be the beginning of a long and mutually beneficial relationship of publishing in Dickens' journals that would eventually reach 73 poems in House words together with a further 7 poems in All the Year Round, most of which were collected and later published into her first two volumes of poetry, both entitled Legends and Lyrics.

Procter was also the editor of the journal Victoria Regia, which became the showpiece of the Victoria Press, a venture hoping to promote the employment of women in all manner of trades and professions.

Procter's health failed in 1862. Dickens and others suggested that this illness was due to her extensive and exhausting schedule of charity work.

An attempt to improve her health by taking a cure at Malvern failed.

Adelaide Anne Proctor died on 3rd February 1864 of tuberculosis. She had been bed-ridden for almost a year. Procter was buried in Kensal Green Cemetery.

Index of Contents

A False Genius
Adelaide Anne Proctor – A Short Biography
Adelaide Anne Proctor – A Concise Bibliography

The Tyrant and the Captive

It was midnight when I listened,
And I heard two Voices speak;
One was harsh, and stern, and cruel,
And the other soft and weak:
Yet I saw no Vision enter,
And I heard no steps depart,
Of this Tyrant and his Captive, . . .
Fate it might be and a Heart.

Thus the stern Voice spake in triumph:—
"I have shut your life away
From the radiant world of nature,
And the perfumed light of day.
You, who loved to steep your spirit
In the charm of Earth's delight,
See no glory of the daytime,
And no sweetness of the night."

But the soft Voice answered calmly:
"Nay, for when the March winds bring
Just a whisper to my window,
I can dream the rest of Spring;
And to-day I saw a Swallow
Flitting past my prison bars,
And my cell has just one corner
Whence at night I see the stars."

But its bitter taunt repeating,
Cried the harsh Voice:—"Where are they–
All the friends of former hours,
Who forget your name to-day?
All the links of love are shattered,
Which you thought so strong before;
And your very heart is lonely,
And alone since loved no more."

But the low Voice spoke still lower:–
"Nay, I know the golden chain
Of my love is purer, stronger,
For the cruel fire of pain:

They remember me no longer,
But I, grieving here alone,
Bind their souls to me for ever
By the love within their own."

But the Voice cried:- "Once remember
You devoted soul and mind
To the welfare of your brethren,
And the service of your kind.
Now, what sorrow can you comfort?
You, who lie in helpless pain,
With an impotent compassion
Fretting out your life in vain."

"Nay;" and then the gentle answer
Rose more loud, and full, and clear:
"For the sake of all my brethren
I thank God that I am here!
Poor had been my Life's best efforts,
Now I waste no thought or breath—
For the prayer of those who suffer
Has the strength of Love and Death."

The Carver's Lesson

Trust me, no mere skill of subtle tracery,
No mere practice of a dexterous hand,
Will suffice, without a hidden spirit,
That we may, or may not, understand.

And those quaint old fragments that are left us
Have their power in this,—the Carver brought
Earnest care, and reverent patience, only
Worthily to clothe some noble thought.

Shut then in the petals of the flowers,
Round the stems of all the lilies twine,
Hide beneath each bird's or angel's pinion,
Some wise meaning or some thought divine.

Place in stony hands that pray for ever
Tender words of peace, and strive to wind
Round the leafy scrolls and fretted niches
Some true, loving message to your kind.

Some will praise, some blame, and, soon forgetting,

Come and go, nor even pause to gaze;
Only now and then a passing stranger
Just may loiter with a word of praise.

But I think, when years have floated onward,
And the stone is grey, and dim, and old,
And the hand forgotten that has carved it,
And the heart that dreamt it still and cold;

There may come some weary soul, o'erladen
With perplexed struggle in his brain,
Or, it may be, fretted with life's turmoil,
Or made sore with some perpetual pain.

Then, I think those stony hands will open,
And the gentle lilies overflow,
With the blessing and the loving token
That you hid there many years ago.

And the tendrils will unroll, and teach him
How to solve the problem of his pain;
And the birds' and angels' wings shake downward
On his heart a sweet and tender rain.

While he marvels at his fancy, reading
Meaning in that quaint and ancient scroll,
Little guessing that the loving Carver
Left a message for his weary soul.

Three Roses

Just when the red June Roses blow
She gave me one,—a year ago.
A Rose whose crimson breath revealed
The secret that its heart concealed,
And whose half shy, half tender grace
Blushed back upon the giver's face.
A year ago—a year ago—
To hope was not to know.

Just when the red June Roses blow
I plucked her one,—a month ago:
Its half-blown crimson to eclipse,
I laid it on her smiling lips;
The balmy fragrance of the south
Drew sweetness from her sweeter mouth.

Swiftly do golden hours creep,–
To hold is not to keep.

The red June Roses now are past,
This very day I broke the last–
And now its perfumed breath is hid,
With her, beneath a coffin-lid;
There will its petals fall apart,
And wither on her icy heart:-
At three red Roses' cost
My world was gained and lost.

My Picture Gallery

I.

You write and think of me, my friend, with pity;
While you are basking in the light of Rome,
Shut up within the heart of this great city,
Too busy and too poor to leave my home.

II.

You think my life debarred all rest or pleasure,
Chained all day to my ledger and my pen;
Too sickly even to use my little leisure
To bear me from the strife and din of men.

III.

Well, it is true; yet, now the days are longer,
At sunset I can lay my writing down,
And slowly crawl (summer has made me stronger)
Just to the nearest outskirt of the town.

IV.

There a wide Common, blackened though and dreary
With factory smoke, spreads outward to the West;
I lie down on the parched-up grass, if weary,
Or lean against a broken wall to rest.

V.

So might a King, turning to Art's rich treasure,
At evening, when the cares of state were done,

Enter his royal gallery, drinking pleasure
Slowly from each great picture, one by one.

VI.

Towards the West I turn my weary spirit,
And watch my pictures: one each night is mine.
Earth and my soul, sick of day's toil, inherit
A portion of that luminous peace divine.

VII.

There I have seen a sunset's crimson glory,
Burn as if earth were one great Altar's blaze;
Or, like the closing of a piteous story,
Light up the misty world with dying rays.

VIII.

There I have seen the Clouds, in pomp and splendour,
Their gold and purple banners all unfurl;
There I have watched colours, more faint and tender
Than pure and delicate tints upon a pearl.

IX.

Skies strewn with roses fading, fading slowly,
While one star trembling watched the daylight die;
Or deep in gloom a sunset, hidden wholly,
Save through gold rents torn in a violet sky.

X.

Or parted clouds, as if asunder riven
By some great angel—and beyond a space
Of far-off tranquil light; the gates of Heaven
Will lead us grandly to as calm a place.

XI.

Or stern dark walls of cloudy mountain ranges
Hid all the wonders that we knew must be;
While, far on high, some little white clouds changes'
Revealed the glory they alone could see.

XII.

Or in wild wrath the affrighted clouds lay shattered,

Like treasures of the lost Hesperides,
All in a wealth of ruined splendour scattered,
Save one strange light on distant silver seas.

XIII.

What land or time can claim the Master Painter,
Whose art could teach him half such gorgeous dyes?
Or skill so rare, but purer hues and fainter
Melt every evening in my western skies.

XIV.

So there I wait, until the shade has lengthened,
And night's blue misty curtain floated down;
Then, with my heart calmed, and my spirit strengthened,
I crawl once more back to the sultry town.

XV.

What Monarch, then, has nobler recreations
Than mine? Or where the great and classic Land
Whose wealth of Art delights the gathered nations
That owns a Picture Gallery half as grand?

Never Again

"Never again!" vow hearts when reunited,
"Never again shall Love be cast aside;
For ever now the shadow has departed;
Nor bitter sorrow, veiled in scornful pride,
Shall feign indifference, or affect disdain,—
Never, oh Love, again, never again!"

"Never again!" so sobs, in broken accents,
A soul laid prostrate at a holy shrine,—
"Once more, once more forgive, oh Lord, and pardon,
My wayward life shall bend to love divine;
And never more shall sin its whiteness stain,—
Never, oh God, again, never again!"

"Never again!" so speaketh one forsaken,
In the blank desolate passion of despair,—
"Never again shall the bright dream I cherished
Delude my heart, for bitter truth is there,—
The angel, Hope, shall still thy cruel pain

Never again, my heart, never again!"

"Never again!" so speaks the sudden silence,
When round the hearth gathers each well-known face,–
But one is missing, and no future presence,
However dear, can fill that vacant place;
For ever shall the burning thought remain,–
"Never, beloved, again! never again!"

"Never again!" so–but beyond our hearing–
Ring out far voices fading up the sky;
Never again shall earthly care and sorrow
Weigh down the wings that bear those souls on high;
Listen, oh earth, and hear that glorious strain,–
"Never, never again! never again!"

Listening Angels

Blue against the bluer Heavens
Stood the mountain, calm and still,
Two white Angels, bending earthward,
Leant upon the hill.
Listening leant those silent Angels,
And I also longed to hear
What sweet strain of earthly music
Thus could charm their ear.
I heard the sound of many trumpets
In a warlike march draw nigh;
Solemnly a mighty army
Passed in order by.
But the clang had ceased; the echoes
Soon had faded from the hill;
While the Angels, calm and earnest,
Leant and listened still.
Then I heard a fainter clamour,
Forge and wheel were clashing near
And the Reapers in the meadow
Singing loud and clear.
When the sunset came in glory,
And the toil of day was o'er,
Still the Angels leant in silence,
Listening as before.
Then, as daylight slowly vanished,
And the evening mists grew dim,
Solemnly from distant voices
Rose a vesper hymn.

When the chant was done, and lingering
Died upon the evening air,
From the hill the radiant Angels
Still were listening there.
Silent came the gathering darkness,
Bringing with it sleep and rest;
Save a little bird was singing
Near her leafy nest.
Through the sounds of war and labour
She had warbled all day long,
While the Angels leant and listened
Only to her song.
But the starry night was coming;
When she ceased her little lay
From the mountain top the Angels
Slowly passed away.

Philip and Mildred

Lingering fade the rays of daylight, and the listening air is chilly;
Voice of bird and forest murmur, insect hum and quivering spray
Stir not in that quiet hour: through the valley, calm and stilly,
All in hushed and loving silence watch the slow departing Day.

Till the last faint western cloudlet, faint and rosy, ceases blushing,
And the blue grows deep and deeper where one trembling planet shines,
And the day has gone for ever—then, like some great ocean rushing,
The sad night wind wails lamenting, sobbing through the moaning pines.

Such, of all day's changing hours, is the fittest and the meetest
For a farewell hour—and parting looks less bitter and more blest;
Earth seems like a shrine for sorrow, Nature's mother voice is sweetest,
And her hand seems laid in chiding on the unquiet throbbing breast.

Words are lower, for the twilight seems rebuking sad repining,
And wild murmur and rebellion, as all childish and in vain;
Breaking through dark future hours clustering starry hopes seem shining,
Then the calm and tender midnight folds her shadow round the pain.

So they paced the shady lime-walk in that twilight dim and holy,
Still the last farewell deferring, she could hear or he should say;
Every word, weighed down by sorrow, fell more tenderly and slowly—
This, which now beheld their parting, should have been their wedding-day.

Should have been: her dreams of childhood, never straying, never faltering,
Still had needed Philip's image to make future life complete;

Philip's young hopes of ambition, ever changing, ever altering,
Needed Mildred's gentle presence even to make successes sweet.

This day should have seen their marriage; the calm crowning and assurance
Of two hearts, fulfilling rather, and not changing, either life:
Now they must be rent asunder, and her heart must learn endurance,
For he leaves their home, and enters on a world of work and strife.

But her gentle spirit long had learnt, unquestioning, submitting,
To revere his youthful longings, and to marvel at the fate
That gave such a humble office, all unworthy and unfitting,
To the genius of the village, who was born for something great.

When the learned Traveller came there who had gained renown at college,
Whose abstruse research had won him even European fame,
Questioned Philip, praised his genius, marvelled at his self-taught knowledge,
Could she murmur if he called him up to London and to fame?

Could she waver when he bade her take the burden of decision,
Since his troth to her was plighted, and his life was now her own?
Could she doom him to inaction? could she, when a newborn vision
Rose in glory for his future, check it for her sake alone?

So her little trembling fingers, that had toiled with such fond pleasure,
Paused, and laid aside, and folded the unfinished wedding gown;
Faltering earnestly assurance, that she too could, in her measure,
Prize for him the present honour, and the future's sure renown.

Now they pace the shady lime-walk, now the last words must be spoken,
Words of trust, for neither dreaded more than waiting and delay;
Was not love still called eternal—could a plighted vow be broken?—
See the crimson light of sunset fades in purple mist away.

"Yes, my Mildred," Philip told her, "one calm thought of joy and blessing,
Like a guardian spirit by me, through the world's tumultuous stir,
Still will spread its wings above me, and now urging, now repressing,
With my Mildred's voice will murmur thoughts of home, and love, and her.

"It will charm my peaceful leisure, sanctify my daily toiling,
With a right none else possesses, touching my heart's inmost string;
And to keep its pure wings spotless I shall fly the world's touch, soiling
Even in thought this Angel Guardian of my Mildred's Wedding Ring.

"Take it, dear; this little circlet is the first link, strong and holy,
Of a life-long chain, and holds me from all other love apart;
Till the day when you may wear it as my wife—my own—mine wholly—
Let me know it rests for ever near the beating of your heart."

Dawn of day saw Philip speeding on his road to the Great City,
Thinking how the stars gazed downward just with Mildred's patient eyes;
Dreams of work, and fame, and honour struggling with a tender pity,
Till the loving Past receding saw the conquering Future rise.

Daybreak still found Mildred watching, with the wonder of first sorrow,
How the outward world unaltered shone the same this very day;
How unpitying and relentless busy life met this new morrow,
Earth, and sky, and man unheeding that her joy had passed away.

Then the round of weary duties, cold and formal, came to meet her,
With the life within departed that had given them each a soul;
And her sick heart even slighted gentle words that came to greet her;
For Grief spread its shadowy pinions, like a blight, upon the whole.

Jar one chord, the harp is silent; move one stone, the arch is shattered;
One small clarion-cry of sorrow bids an armed host awake;
One dark cloud can hide the sunlight; loose one string, the pearls are scattered;
Think one thought, a soul may perish; say one word, a heart may break!

Life went on, the two lives running side by side; the outward seeming,
And the truer and diviner hidden in the heart and brain;
Dreams grow holy, put in action; work grows fair through starry dreaming;
But where each flows on unmingling, both are fruitless and in vain.

Such was Mildred's life; her dreaming lay in some far-distant region,
All the fairer, all the brighter, that its glories were but guessed;
And the daily round of duties seemed an unreal, airy legion—
Nothing true save Philip's letters and the ring upon her breast.

Letters telling how he struggled, for some plan or vision aiming,
And at last how he just grasped it as a fresh one spread its wings;
How the honour or the learning, once the climax, now were claiming,
Only more and more, becoming merely steps to higher things.

Telling her of foreign countries: little store had she of learning,
So her earnest, simple spirit answered as he touched the string;
Day by day, to these bright fancies all her silent thoughts were turning,
Seeing every radiant picture framed within her golden Ring.

Oh, poor heart—love, if thou willest; but, thine own soul still possessing,
Live thy life: not a reflection or a shadow of his own:
Lean as fondly, as completely, as thou willest—but confessing
That thy strength is God's, and therefore can, if need be, stand alone.

Little means were there around her to make farther, wider ranges,
Where her loving gentle spirit could try any stronger flight;
And she turned aside, half fearing that fresh thoughts were fickle changes—

That she must stay as he left her on that farewell summer night.

Love should still be guide and leader, like a herald should have risen,
Lighting up the long dark vistas, conquering all opposing fates;
But new claims, new thoughts, new duties found her heart a silent prison,
And found Love, with folded pinions, like a jailer by the gates.

Yet why blame her? it had needed greater strength than she was given
To have gone against the current that so calmly flowed along;
Nothing fresh came near the village save the rain and dew of heaven,
And her nature was too passive, and her love perhaps too strong.

The great world of thought, that rushes down the years, and onward sweeping
Bears upon its mighty billows in its progress each and all,
Flowed so far away, its murmur did not rouse them from their sleeping;
Life and Time and Truth were speaking, but they did not hear their call.

Years flowed on; and every morning heard her prayer grow lower, deeper,
As she called all blessings on him, and bade every ill depart,
And each night when the cold moonlight shone upon that quiet sleeper,
It would show her ring that glittered with each throbbing of her heart.

Years passed on. Fame came for Philip in a full, o'erflowing measure;
He was spoken of and honoured through the breadth of many lands,
And he wrote it all to Mildred, as if praise were only pleasure,
As if fame were only honour, when he laid them in her hands.

Mildred heard it without wonder, as a sure result expected,
For how could it fail, since merit and renown go side by side:
And the neighbours who first fancied genius ought to be suspected,
Might at last give up their caution, and could own him now with pride.

Years flowed on. These empty honours led to others they called better,
He had saved some slender fortune, and might claim his bride at last:
Mildred, grown so used to waiting, felt half startled by the letter
That now made her future certain, and would consecrate her past.

And he came: grown sterner, older—changed indeed: a grave reliance
Had replaced his eager manner, and the quick short speech of old:
He had gone forth with a spirit half of hope and half defiance;
He returned with proud assurance half disdainful and half cold.

Yet his old self seemed returning while he stood sometimes, and listened
To her calm soft voice, relating all the thoughts of these long years;
And if Mildred's heart was heavy, and at times her blue eyes glistened,
Still in thought she would not whisper aught of sorrow or of fears.

Autumn with its golden corn-fields, autumn with its storms and showers,

Had been there to greet his coming with its forests gold and brown;
And the last leaves still were falling, fading still the year's last flowers,
When he left the quiet village, and took back his bride to town.

Home—the home that she had pictured many a time in twilight, dwelling
On that tender gentle fancy, folded round with loving care;
Here was home—the end, the haven; and what spirit voice seemed telling,
That she only held the casket, with the gem no longer there?

Sad it may be to be longing, with a patience faint and weary,
For a hope deferred—and sadder still to see it fade and fall;
Yet to grasp the thing we long for, and, with sorrow sick and dreary,
Then to find how it can fail us, is the saddest pain of all.

What was wanting? He was gentle, kind, and generous still, deferring
To her wishes always; nothing seemed to mar their tranquil life:
There are skies so calm and leaden that we long for storm-winds stirring,
There is peace so cold and bitter, that we almost welcome strife.

Darker grew the clouds above her, and the slow conviction clearer,
That he gave her home and pity, but that heart, and soul, and mind
Were beyond her now; he loved her, and in youth he had been near her,
But he now had gone far onward, and had left her there behind.

Yes, beyond her: yes, quick-hearted, her Love helped her in revealing
It was worthless, while so mighty; was too weak, although so strong;
There were courts she could not enter; depths she could not sound; yet feeling
It was vain to strive or struggle, vainer still to mourn or long.

He would give her words of kindness, he would talk of home, but seeming
With an absent look, forgetting if he held or dropped her hand;
And then turn with eager pleasure to his writing, reading, dreaming,
Or to speak of things with others that she could not understand.

He had paid, and paid most nobly, all he owed; no need of blaming;
It had cost him something, may be, that no future could restore:
In her heart of hearts she knew it; Love and Sorrow, not complaining,
Only suffered all the deeper, only loved him all the more.

Sometimes then a stronger anguish, and more cruel, weighed upon her,
That through all those years of waiting, he had slowly learnt the truth;
He had known himself mistaken, but that, bound to her in honour,
He renounced his life, to pay her for the patience of her youth.

But a star was slowly rising from that mist of grief, and brighter
Grew her eyes, for each slow hour surer comfort seemed to bring;
And she watched with strange sad smiling, how her trembling hands grew slighter,
And how thin her slender finger, and how large her wedding-ring.

And the tears dropped slowly on it, as she kissed that golden token
With a deeper love, it may be, than was in the far-off past;
And remembering Philip's fancy, that so long ago was spoken,
Thought her Ring's bright angel guardian had stayed near her to the last.

Grieving sorely, grieving truly, with a tender care and sorrow,
Philip watched the slow, sure fading of his gentle, patient wife;
Could he guess with what a yearning she was longing for the morrow,
Could he guess the bitter knowledge that had wearied her of life?

Now with violets strewn upon her, Mildred lies in peaceful sleeping;
All unbound her long, bright tresses, and her throbbing heart at rest,
And the cold, blue rays of moonlight, through the open casement creeping,
Show the ring upon her finger, and her hands crossed on her breast.

Peace at last. Of peace eternal is her calm sweet smile a token.
Has some angel lingering near her let a radiant promise fall?
Has he told her Heaven unites again the links that Earth has broken?
For on Earth so much is needed, but in Heaven Love is all!

Borrowed Thoughts

I. FROM "LAVATER."

Trust him little who doth raise
To one height both great and small,
And sets the sacred crown of praise,
Smiling, on the head of all.

Trust him less who looks around
To censure all with scornful eyes,
And in everything has found
Something that he dare despise.

But for one who stands apart,
Stirred by nought that can befall,
With a cold indifferent heart,–
Trust him least and last of all.

II. FROM "PHANTASTES."

I have a bitter Thought, a Snake
That used to sting my life to pain.
I strove to cast it far away,

But every night and every day
It crawled back to my heart again.

It was in vain to live or strive,
To think or sleep, to work or pray;
At last I bade this thine accursed
Gnaw at my heart, and do its worst,
And so I let it have its way.

Thus said I, "I shall never fall
Into a false and dreaming peace,
And then awake, with sudden start,
To feel it biting at my heart,
For now the pain can never cease."

But I gained more; for I have found
That such a snake's envenomed charm
Must always, always find a part,
Deep in the centre of my heart,
Which it can never wound or harm.

It is coiled round my heart to-day.
It sleeps at times, this cruel snake,
And while it sleeps it never stings:-
Hush! let us talk of other things,
Lest it should hear me and awake.

III. FROM "LOST ALICE."

Yes, dear, our Love is slain;
In the cold grave for evermore it lies,
Never to wake again,
Or light our sorrow with its starry eyes;
And so—regret is vain.

One hour of pain and dread,
We killed our Love, we took its life away
With the false words we said;
And so we watch it, since that cruel day,
Silent, and cold, and dead.

We should have seen it shine
Long years beside us. Time and Death might try
To touch that life divine,
Whose strength could every other stroke defy
Save only thine and mine.

No longing can restore
Our dead again. Vain are the tears we weep,
And vainly we deplore
Our buried Love: its grave lies dark and deep
Between us evermore.

IV. FROM —

Within the kingdom of my Soul
I bid you enter, Love, to-day;
Submit my life to your control,
And give my Heart up to your sway.

My Past, whose light and life is flown,
Shall live through memory for you still;
Take all my Present for your own,
And mould my Future to your will.

One only thought remains apart,
And will for ever so remain;
There is one Chamber in my heart
Where even you might knock in vain.

A haunted Chamber:- long ago
I closed it, and I cast the key
Where deep and bitter waters flow,
Into a vast and silent sea.

Dear, it is haunted. All the rest
Is yours; but I have shut that door
For ever now. 'Tis even best
That I should enter it no more.

No more. It is not well to stay
With ghosts; their very look would scare
Your joyous, loving smile away—
So never try to enter there.

Check, if you love me, all regret
That this one thought remains apart:-
Now let us smile, dear, and forget
The haunted Chamber in my Heart.

Light and Shade

Thou hast done well to kneel and say,
"Since He who gave can take away,
And bid me suffer, I obey."

And also well to tell thy heart
That good lies in the bitterest part,
And thou wilt profit by her smart.

But bitter hours come to all:
When even truths like these will pall,
Sick hearts for humbler comfort call.

Then I would have thee strive to see
That good and evil come to thee,
As one of a great family.

And as material life is planned,
That even the loneliest one must stand
Dependent on his brother's hand;

So links more subtle and more fine
Bind every other soul to thine
In one great brotherhood divine.

Nor with thy share of work be vexed;
Though incomplete, and even perplex,
It fits exactly to the next.

What seems so dark to thy dim sight
May be a shadow, seen aright,
Making some brightness doubly bright.

The flash that struck thy tree,—no more
To shelter thee,—lets Heaven's blue floor
Shine where it never shone before.

Thy life that has been dropped aside
Into Time's stream, may stir the tide,
In rippled circles spreading wide.

The cry wrung from thy spirit's pain
May echo on some far-off plain,
And guide a wanderer home again.

Fail—yet rejoice; because no less
The failure that makes thy distress
May teach another full success.

It may be that in some great need
Thy life's poor fragments are decreed
To help build up a lofty deed.

Thy heart should throb in vast content,
Thus knowing that it was but meant
As chord in one great instrument;

That even the discord in thy soul
May make completer music roll
From out the great harmonious whole.

It may be, that when all is light,
Deep set within that deep delight
Will be to know why all was right;

To hear life's perfect music rise,
And while it floods the happy skies,
Thy feeble voice to recognise.

Then strive more gladly to fulfil
Thy little part. This darkness still
Is light to every loving will.

And trust,—as if already plain,
How just thy share of loss and pain
Is for another fuller gain.

I dare not limit time or place
Touched by thy life: nor dare I trace
Its far vibrations into space.

One only knows. Yet if the fret
Of thy weak heart, in weak regret
Needs a more tender comfort yet:

Then thou mayst take thy loneliest fears,
The bitterest drops of all thy tears,
The dreariest hours of all thy years;

And through thy anguish there outspread,
May ask that God's great love would shed
Blessings on one beloved head.

And thus thy soul shall learn to draw
Sweetness from out that loving law
That sees no failure and no flaw,

Where all is good. And life is good,
Were the one lesson understood
Of its most sacred brotherhood.

A Changeling

A little changeling spirit
Crept to my arms one day:
I had no heart or courage
To drive the child away.

So all day long I soothed her,
And hushed her on my breast;
And all night long her wailing
Would never let me rest.

I dug a grave to hold her,
A grave both dark and deep;
I covered her with violets,
And laid her there to sleep.

I used to go and watch there,
Both night and morning too:-
It was my tears, I fancy,
That kept the violets blue.

I took her up: and once more
I felt the clinging hold,
And heard the ceaseless wailing
That wearied me of old.

I wandered, and I wandered,
With my burden on my breast,
Till I saw a church-door open,
And entered in to rest.

In the dim, dying daylight,
Set in a flowery shrine,
I saw the Virgin Mother
Holding her Child divine.

I knelt down there in silence,
And on the Altar-stone
I laid my wailing burden,
And came away—alone.

And now that little spirit,
That sobbed so all day long,
Is grown a shining Angel,
With wines both wide and strong.

She watches me from Heaven,
With loving, tender care,
And one day she has promised
That I shall find her there.

Discouraged

Where the little babbling streamlet
First springs forth to light,
Trickling through soft velvet mosses,
Almost hid from sight;
Vowed I with delight,—
"River, I will follow thee,
Through thy wanderings to the Sea!"

Gleaming 'mid the purple heather,
Downward then it sped,
Glancing through the mountain gorges,
Like a silver thread,
As it quicker fled,
Louder music in its flow,
Dashing to the Vale below.

Then its voice grew lower, gentler,
And its pace less fleet,
Just as though it loved to linger
Round the rushes' feet,
As they stooped to meet
Their clear images below,
Broken by the ripples' flow.

Purple Willow-herb bent over
To her shadow fair;
Meadow-sweet, in feathery clusters,
Perfumed all the air;
Silver-weed was there,
And in one calm, grassy spot,
Starry, blue Forget-me-not.

Tangled weeds, below the waters,
Still seemed drawn away;
Yet the current, floating onward,

Was less strong than they;–
Sunbeams watched their play,
With a flickering light and shade,
Through the screen the Alders made.

Broader grew the flowing River;
To its grassy brink
Slowly, in the slanting sun-rays,
Cattle trooped to drink:
The blue sky, I think,
Was no bluer than that stream,
Slipping onward, like a dream.

Quicker, deeper then it hurried,
Rushing fierce and free;
But I said, "It should grow calmer
Ere it meets the Sea,
The wide purple Sea,
Which I weary for in vain,
Wasting all my toil and pain."

But it rushed still quicker, fiercer,
In its rocky bed,
Hard and stony was the pathway
To my tired tread;
"I despair," I said,
"Of that wide and glorious Sea
That was promised unto me."

So I turned aside, and wandered
Through green meadows near,
Far away, among the daisies,
Far away, for fear
Lest I still should hear
The loud murmur of its song,
As the River flowed along.

Now I hear it not:- I loiter
Gaily as before;
Yet I sometimes think,–and thinking
Makes my heart so sore,–
Just a few steps more,
And there might have shone for me,
Blue and infinite, the Sea.

If Thou Couldst Know

I think if thou couldst know,
Oh soul that will complain,
What lies concealed below
Our burden and our pain;
How just our anguish brings
Nearer those longed-for things
We seek for now in vain,—
I think thou wouldst rejoice, and not complain.

I think if thou couldst see,
With thy dim mortal sight,
How meanings, dark to thee,
Are shadows hiding light;
Truth's efforts crossed and vexed,
Life's purpose all perplexed,—
If thou couldst see them right,
I think that they would seem all clear, and wise, and bright.

And yet thou canst not know,
And yet thou canst not see;
Wisdom and sight are slow
In poor humanity.
If thou couldst trust, poor soul,
In Him who rules the whole,
Thou wouldst find peace and rest:
Wisdom and sight are well, but Trust is best.

The Warrior To His Dead Bride

If in the fight my arm was strong,
And forced my foes to yield,
If conquering and unhurt I came
Back from the battle-field—
It is because thy prayers have been
My safeguard and my shield.

My comrades smile to see my arm
Spare or protect a foe,
They think thy gentle pleading voice
Was silenced long ago;
But pity and compassion, love,
Were taught me first by woe.

Thy heart, my own, still beats in Heaven
With the same love divine

That made thee stoop to such a soul,
So hard, so stern, as mine–
My eyes have learnt to weep, beloved,
Since last they looked on thine.

I hear thee murmur words of peace
Through the dim midnight air,
And a calm falls from the angel stars
And soothes my great despair–
The Heavens themselves look brighter, love,
Since thy sweet soul is there.

And if my heart is once more calm,
My step is once more free,
It is because each hour I feel
Thou prayest still for me;
Because no fate or change can come
Between my soul and thee.

It is because my heart is stilled.
Not broken by despair,
Because I see the grave is bright,
And death itself is fair–
I dread no more the wrath of Heaven–
I have an angel there!

A Comforter

I.

Will she come to me, little Effie,
Will she come in my arms to rest,
And nestle her head on my shoulder,
While the sun goes down in the west?

II.

"I and Effie will sit together,
All alone, in this great arm-chair:-
Is it silly to mind it, darling,
When Life is so hard to bear?

III.

"No one comforts me like my Effie,
Just I think that she does not try,–

Only looks with a wistful wonder
Why grown people should ever cry;

IV.

"While her little soft arms close tighter
Round my neck in their clinging hold:-
Well, I must not cry on your hair, dear,
For my tears might tarnish the gold.

V.

"I am tired of trying to read, dear;
It is worse to talk and seem gay:
There are some kinds of sorrow, Effie,
It is useless to thrust away.

VI.

"Ah, advice may be wise, my darling,
But one always knows it before;
And the reasoning down one's sorrow
Seems to make one suffer the more.

VII.

"But my Effie won't reason, will she?
Or endeavour to understand;
Only holds up her mouth to kiss me,
As she strokes my face with her hand.

VIII.

"If you break your plaything yourself, dear,
Don't you cry for it all the same?
I don't think it is such a comfort,
One has only oneself to blame.

IX.

"People say things cannot be helped, dear,
But then that is the reason why;
For if things could be helped or altered,
One would never sit down to cry:

X.

"They say, too, that tears are quite useless

To undo, amend, or restore,—
When I think how useless, my Effie,
Then my tears only fall the more.

XI.

"All to-day I struggled against it;
But that does not make sorrow cease;
And now, dear, it is such a comfort
To be able to cry in peace.

XII.

"Though wise people would call that folly,
And remonstrate with grave surprise;
We won't mind what they say, my Effie;—
We never professed to be wise.

"But my comforter knows a lesson
Wiser, truer than all the rest:-
That to help and to heal a sorrow,
Love and silence are always best.

XIV.

"Well, who is my comforter—tell me?
Effie smiles, but she will not speak;
Or look up through the long curled lashes
That are shading her rosy cheek.

XV.

"Is she thinking of talking fishes,
The blue bird, or magical tree?
Perhaps I am thinking, my darling,
Of something that never can be.

XVI.

"You long—don't you, dear?—for the Genii,
Who were slaves of lamps and of rings;
And I—I am sometimes afraid, dear,—
I want as impossible things.

XVII.

"But hark! there is Nurse calling Effie!
It is bedtime, so run away;

And I must go back, or the others
Will be wondering why I stay.

XVIII.

"So good-night to my darling Effie;
Keep happy, sweetheart, and grow wise:-
There's one kiss for her golden tresses,
And two for her sleepy eyes."

Unseen

There are more things in Heaven and Earth, than we
Can dream of, or than nature understands;
We learn not through our poor philosophy
What hidden chords are touched by unseen hands.
The present hour repeats upon its strings
Echoes of some vague dream we have forgot;
Dim voices whisper half-remembered things,
And when we pause to listen,–answer not.
Forebodings come: we know not how, or whence,
Shadowing a nameless fear upon the soul,
And stir within our hearts a subtler sense,
Than light may read, or wisdom may control.
And who can tell what secret links of thought
Bind heart to heart? Unspoken things are heard,
As if within our deepest selves was brought
The soul, perhaps, of some unuttered word.
But, though a veil of shadow hangs between
That hidden life, and what we see and hear,
Let us revere the power of the Unseen,
And know a world of mystery is near.

A Remembrance of Autumn

Nothing stirs the sunny silence,–
Save the drowsy humming of the bees
Round the rich, ripe peaches on the wall,
And the south wind sighing in the trees,
And the dead leaves rustling as they fall:
While the swallows, one by one, are gathering,
All impatient to be on the wing,
And to wander from us, seeking
Their beloved Spring!

Cloudless rise the azure heavens!
Only vaporous wreaths of snowy white
Nestle in the grey hill's rugged side;
And the golden woods are bathed in light,
Dying, if they must, with kingly pride:
While the swallows in the blue air wheeling,
Circle now an eager fluttering band,
Ready to depart and leave us
For a brighter land!

But a voice is sounding sadly,
Telling of a glory that has been;
Of a day that faded all too fast—
See afar through the blue air serene,
Where the swallows wing their way at last,
And our hearts perchance, as sadly wandering,
Vainly seeking for a long-lost day,
While we watch the far-off swallows,
Flee with them away!

Three Evenings in a Life aka Three Evenings in the House

FIRST EVENING

I.

Yes, it looked dark and dreary,
That long and narrow street:
Only the sound of the rain,
And the tramp of passing feet,
The duller glow of the fire,
And gathering mists of night
To mark how slow and weary
The long day's cheerless flight!

II.

Watching the sullen fire,
Hearing the dismal rain,
Drop after drop, run down
On the darkening window-pane:
Chill was the heart of Alice,
Chill as that winter day,—
For the star of her life had risen
Only to fade away.

III.

The voice that had been so strong
To bid the snare depart,
The true and earnest will,
The calm and steadfast heart,
Were now weighed down by sorrow,
Were quivering now with pain;
The clear path now seemed clouded,
And all her grief in vain.

IV.

Duty, Right, Truth, who promised
To help and save their own,
Seemed spreading wide their pinions
To leave her there alone.
So, turning from the Present
To well-known days of yore,
She called on them to strengthen
And guard her soul once more.

V.

She thought how in her girlhood
Her life was given away,
The solemn promise spoken
She kept so well to-day;
How to her brother Herbert
She had been help and guide,
And how his artist nature
On her calm strength relied.

VI.

How through life's fret and turmoil
The passion and fire of art
In him was soothed and quickened
By her true sister heart;
How future hopes had always
Been for his sake alone;
And now,—what strange new feeling
Possessed her as its own?

VII.

Her home—each flower that breathed there,
The wind's sigh, soft and low,
Each trembling spray of ivy,

The river's murmuring flow,
The shadow of the forest,
Sunset, or twilight dim—
Dear as they were, were dearer
By leaving them for him.

VIII.

And each year as it found her
In the dull, feverish town,
Saw self still more forgotten,
And selfish care kept down
By the calm joy of evening
That brought him to her side,
To warn him with wise counsel,
Or praise with tender pride.

IX.

Her heart, her life, her future,
Her genius, only meant
Another thing to give him,
And be therewith content.
To-day, what words had stirred her,
Her soul could not forget?
What dream had filled her spirit
With strange and wild regret?

X.

To leave him for another,—
Could it indeed be so?
Could it have cost such anguish
To bid this vision go?
Was this her faith? Was Herbert
The second in her heart?
Did it need all this struggle
To bid a dream depart?

XI.

And yet, within her spirit
A far-off land was seen,
A home, which might have held her,
A love, which might have been.
And Life—not the mere being
Of daily ebb and flow,
But Life itself had claimed her,

And she had let it go!

XII.

Within her heart there echoed
Again the well-known tone
That promised this bright future,
And asked her for her own:
Then words of sorrow, broken
By half-reproachful pain;
And then a farewell spoken
In words of cold disdain.

XIII.

Where now was the stern purpose
That nerved her soul so long?
Whence came the words she uttered,
So hard, so cold, so strong?
What right had she to banish
A hope that God had given?
Why must she choose earth's portion,
And turn aside from Heaven?

XIV.

To-day! Was it this morning?
If this long, fearful strife
Was but the work of hours,
What would be years of life?
Why did a cruel Heaven
For such great suffering call?
And why—Oh, still more cruel!—
Must her own words do all?

XV.

Did she repent? Oh Sorrow!
Why do we linger still
To take thy loving message,
And do thy gentle will?
See, her tears fall more slowly,
The passionate murmurs cease,
And back upon her spirit
Flow strength, and love, and peace.

XVI.

The fire burns more brightly,
The rain has passed away,
Herbert will see no shadow
Upon his home to-day;
Only that Alice greets him
With doubly tender care,
Kissing a fonder blessing
Down on his golden hair.

SECOND EVENING

I.

The studio is deserted,
Palette and brush laid by,
The sketch rests on the easel,
The paint is scarcely dry;
And Silence—who seems always
Within her depths to bear
The next sound that will utter—
Now holds a dumb despair.

II.

So Alice feels it: listening
With breathless, stony fear,
Waiting the dreadful summons
Each minute brings more near:
When the young life, now ebbing,
Shall fail, and pass away
Into that mighty shadow
Who shrouds the house to-day.

III.

But why—when the sick chamber
Is on the upper floor—
Why dares not Alice enter
Within the close–shut door?
If he—her all—her Brother,
Lies dying in that gloom,
What strange mysterious power
Has sent her from the room?

IV.

It is not one week's anguish
That can have changed her so;
Joy has not died here lately,
Struck down by one quick blow;
But cruel months have needed
Their long relentless chain,
To teach that shrinking manner
Of helpless, hopeless pain.

V.

The struggle was scarce over
Last Christmas Eve had brought:
The fibres still were quivering
Of the one wounded thought,
When Herbert—who, unconscious,
Had guessed no inward strife—
Bade her, in pride and pleasure,
Welcome his fair young wife.

VI.

Bade her rejoice, and smiling,
Although his eyes were dim,
Thanked God he thus could pay her
The care she gave to him.
This fresh bright life would bring her
A new and joyous fate—
Oh, Alice, check the murmur
That cries, "Too late! too late!"

VII.

Too late! Could she have known it
A few short weeks before,
That his life was completed,
And needing hers no more,
She might—Oh sad repining!
What "might have been," forget;
"It was not," should suffice us
To stifle vain regret.

VIII.

He needed her no longer,
Each day it grew more plain;
First with a startled wonder,
Then with a wondering pain.

Love: why, his wife best gave it;
Comfort: durst Alice speak,
Or counsel, when resentment
Flushed on the young wife's cheek?

IX.

No more long talks by firelight
Of childish times long past,
And dreams of future greatness
Which he must reach at last;
Dreams, where her purer instinct
With truth unerring told,
Where was the worthless gilding,
And where refined gold.

X.

Slowly, but surely ever,
Dora's poor jealous pride,
Which she called love for Herbert,
Drove Alice from his side;
And, spite of nervous effort
To share their altered life,
She felt a check to Herbert,
A burden to his wife.

XI.

This was the least; for Alice
Feared, dreaded, knew at length
How much his nature owed her
Of truth, and power, and strength;
And watched the daily failing
Of all his nobler part:
Low aims, weak purpose, telling
In lower, weaker art.

XII.

And now, when he is dying,
The last words she could hear
Must not be hers, but given
The bride of one short year.
The last care is another's;
The last prayer must not be
The one they learnt together
Beside their mother's knee.

XIII.

Summoned at last: she kisses
The clay-cold stiffening hand;
And, reading pleading efforts
To make her understand,
Answers, with solemn promise,
In clear but trembling tone,
To Dora's life henceforward
She will devote her own.

XIV.

Now all is over. Alice
Dares not remain to weep,
But soothes the frightened Dora
Into a sobbing sleep.
The poor weak child will need her: . . .
Oh, who can dare complain,
When God sends a new Duty
To comfort each new Pain!

THIRD EVENING

I.

The House is all deserted,
In the dim evening gloom,
Only one figure passes
Slowly from room to room;
And, pausing at each doorway,
Seems gathering up again
Within her heart the relics
Of bygone joy and pain.

II.

There is an earnest longing
In those who onward gaze,
Looking with weary patience
Towards the coming days.
There is a deeper longing,
More sad, more strong, more keen:
Those know it who look backward,
And yearn for what has been.

III.

At every hearth she pauses,
Touches each well-known chair;
Gazes from every window,
Lingers on every stair.
What have these months brought Alice
Now one more year is past?
This Christmas Eve shall tell us,
The third one and the last.

IV.

The wilful, wayward Dora,
In those first weeks of grief,
Could seek and find in Alice
Strength, soothing, and relief;
And Alice—last sad comfort
True woman-heart can take—
Had something still to suffer
And bear for Herbert's sake.

V.

Spring, with her western breezes,
From Indian islands bore
To Alice news that Leonard
Would seek his home once more.
What was it—joy, or sorrow?
What were they—hopes, or fears?
That flushed her cheeks with crimson,
And filled her eyes with tears?

VI.

He came. And who so kindly
Could ask and hear her tell
Herbert's last hours; for Leonard
Had known and loved him well.
Daily he came; and Alice,
Poor weary heart, at length,
Weighed down by others' weakness,
Could lean upon his strength.

VII.

Yet not the voice of Leonard

Could her true care beguile,
That turned to watch, rejoicing
Dora's reviving smile.
So, from that little household
The worst gloom passed away,
The one bright hour of evening
Lit up the livelong day.

VIII.

Days passed. The golden summer
In sudden heat bore down
Its blue, bright, glowing sweetness
Upon the scorching town.
And sighs and sounds of country
Came in the warm soft tune
Sung by the honeyed breezes
Borne on the wings of June.

IX.

One twilight hour, but earlier
Than usual, Alice thought
She knew the fresh sweet fragrance
Of flowers that Leonard brought;
Through opened doors and windows
It stole up through the gloom,
And with appealing sweetness
Drew Alice from her room.

X.

Yes, he was there; and pausing
Just near the opened door,
To check her heart's quick beating,
She heard—and paused still more—
His low voice—Dora's answers—
His pleading—Yes, she knew
The tone—the words—the accents:
She once had heard them too.

XI.

"Would Alice blame her?" Leonard's
Low, tender answer came;—
"Alice was far too noble
To think or dream of blame."
"And was he sure he loved her?"

"Yes, with the one love given
Once in a lifetime only,
With one soul and one heaven!"

XII.

Then came a plaintive murmur,–
"Dora had once been told
That he and Alice"–"Dearest,
Alice is far too cold
To love; and I, my Dora,
If once I fancied so,
It was a brief delusion,
And over,–long ago."

XIII.

Between the Past and Present,
On that bleak moment's height,
She stood. As some lost traveller
By a quick flash of light
Seeing a gulf before him,
With dizzy, sick despair,
Reels backward, but to find it
A deeper chasm there.

XIV.

The twilight grew still darker,
The fragrant flowers more sweet,
The stars shone out in heaven,
The lamps gleamed down the street;
And hours passed in dreaming
Over their new-found fate,
Ere they could think of wondering
Why Alice was so late.

XV.

She came, and calmly listened;
In vain they strove to trace
If Herbert's memory shadowed
In grief upon her face.
No blame, no wonder showed there,
No feeling could be told;
Her voice was not less steady,
Her manner not more cold.

XVI.

They could not hear the anguish
That broke in words of pain
Through the calm summer midnight,—
"My Herbert—mine again!"
Yes, they have once been parted,
But this day shall restore
The long lost one: she claims him:
"My Herbert—mine once more!"

XVII.

Now Christmas Eve returning,
Saw Alice stand beside
The altar, greeting Dora,
Again a smiling bride;
And now the gloomy evening
Sees Alice pale and worn,
Leaving the house for ever,
To wander out forlorn.

XVIII.

Forlorn—nay, not so. Anguish
Shall do its work at length;
Her soul, passed through the fire,
Shall gain still purer strength.
Somewhere there waits for Alice
An earnest noble part;
And, meanwhile God is with her,—
God, and her own true heart!

An Ideal

While the grey mists of early dawn
Were lingering round the hill,
And the dew was still upon the flowers,
And the earth lay calm and still,
A winged Spirit came to me
Noble, and radiant, and free.

Folding his blue and shining wings,
He laid his hand on mine.
I know not if I felt, or heard
The mystic word divine,

Which woke the trembling air to sighs,
And shone from out his starry eyes.

The word he spoke, within my heart
Stirred life unknown before,
And cast a spell upon my soul
To chain it evermore;
Making the cold dull earth look bright,
And skies flame out in sapphire light.

When noon ruled from the heavens, and man
Through busy day toiled on,
My Spirit drooped his shining wings;
His radiant smile was gone;
His voice had ceased, his grace had flown,
His hand grew cold within my own.

Bitter, oh bitter tears, I wept,
Yet still I held his hand,
Hoping with vague unreasoning hope:
I would not understand
That this pale Spirit never more
Could be what he had been before.

Could it be so? My heart stood still.
Yet he was by my side.
I strove; but my despair was vain;
Vain, too, was love and pride.
Could he have changed to me so soon?
My day was only at its noon.

Now stars are rising one by one,
Through the dim evening air;
Near me a household Spirit waits,
With tender loving care;
He speaks and smiles, but never sings,
Long since he lost his shining wings.

With thankful, true content, I know
This is the better way;
Is not a faithful spirit mine—
Mine still—at close of day? . . .
Yet will my foolish heart repine
For that bright morning dream of mine.

Our Dead

Nothing is our own: we hold our pleasures
Just a little while, ere they are fled:
One by one life robs us of our treasures;
Nothing is our own except our Dead.

They are ours, and hold in faithful keeping
Safe for ever, all they took away.
Cruel life can never stir that sleeping,
Cruel time can never seize that prey.

Justice pales; truth fades; stars fall from Heaven;
Human are the great whom we revere:
No true crown of honour can be given,
Till we place it on a funeral bier.

How the Children leave us: and no traces
Linger of that smiling angel band;
Gone, for ever gone; and in their places,
Weary men and anxious women stand.

Yet we have some little ones, still ours;
They have kept the baby smile we know,
Which we kissed one day and hid with flowers,
On their dead white faces, long ago.

When our Joy is lost—and life will take it—
Then no memory of the past remains;
Save with some strange, cruel sting, to make it
Bitterness beyond all present pains.

Death, more tender-hearted, leaves to sorrow
Still the radiant shadow, fond regret:
We shall find, in some far, bright to-morrow,
Joy that he has taken, living yet.

Is Love ours, and do we dream we know it,
Bound with all our heart-strings, all our own?
Any cold and cruel dawn may show it,
Shattered, desecrated, overthrown.

Only the dead Hearts forsake us never;
Death's last kiss has been the mystic sign
Consecrating Love our own for ever,
Crowning it eternal and divine.

So when Fate would fain besiege our city,
Dim our gold, or make our flowers fall,

Death the Angel, comes in love and pity,
And to save our treasures, claims them all.

FOUNDED ON AN OLD FRENCH LEGEND

The fettered Spirits linger
In purgatorial pain,
With penal fires effacing
Their last faint earthly stain,
Which Life's imperfect sorrow
Had tried to cleanse in vain.

Yet on each feast of Mary
Their sorrow finds release,
For the Great Archangel Michael
Comes down and bids it cease;
And the name of these brief respites
Is called "Our Lady's Peace."

Yet once—so runs the Legend—
When the Archangel came
And all these holy spirits
Rejoiced at Mary's name;
One voice alone was wailing,
Still wailing on the same.

And though a great Te Deum
The happy echoes woke,
This one discordant wailing
Through the sweet voices broke;
So when St. Michael questioned,
Thus the poor spirit spoke:-

"I am not cold or thankless,
Although I still complain;
I prize our Lady's blessing
Although it comes in vain
To still my bitter anguish,
Or quench my ceaseless pain.

"On earth a heart that loved me,
Still lives and mourns me there,
And the shadow of his anguish
Is more than I can bear;

All the torment that I suffer
Is the thought of his despair.

"The evening of my bridal
Death took my Life away;
Not all Love's passionate pleading
Could gain an hour's delay.
And he I left has suffered
A whole year since that day.

"If I could only see him,–
If I could only go
And speak one word of comfort
And solace,–then, I know
He would endure with patience,
And strive against his woe."

Thus the Archangel answered:-
"Your time of pain is brief,
And soon the peace of Heaven
Will give you full relief;
Yet if his earthly comfort
So much outweighs your grief,

"Then, through a special mercy
I offer you this grace,–
You may seek him who mourns you
And look upon his face,
And speak to him of comfort
For one short minute's space.

"But when that time is ended,
Return here, and remain
A thousand years in torment,
A thousand years in pain:
Thus dearly must you purchase
The comfort he will gain."

* * *

The Lime-trees' shade at evening
Is spreading broad and wide;
Beneath their fragrant arches,
Pace slowly, side by side,
In low and tender converse,
A Bridegroom and his Bride.

The night is calm and stilly,

No other sound is there
Except their happy voices:
What is that cold bleak air
That passes through the Lime-trees
And stirs the Bridegroom's hair?

While one low cry of anguish,
Like the last dying wail
Of some dumb, hunted creature,
Is borne upon the gale:-
Why does the Bridegroom shudder
And turn so deathly pale?

* * *

Near Purgatory's entrance
The radiant Angels wait;
It was the great St. Michael
Who closed that gloomy gate,
When the poor wandering spirit
Came back to meet her fate.

* * *

"Pass on," thus spoke the Angel:
"Heaven's joy is deep and vast;
Pass on, pass on, poor Spirit,
For Heaven is yours at last;
In that one minute's anguish
Your thousand years have passed."

A Contrast

Can you open that ebony Casket?
Look, this is the key: but stay,
Those are only a few old letters
Which I keep,—to burn some day.

Yes, that Locket is quaint and ancient;
But leave it, dear, with the ring,
And give me the little Portrait
Which hangs by a crimson string.

I have never opened that Casket
Since, many long years ago,
It was sent me back in anger

By one whom I used to know.

But I want you to see the Portrait:
I wonder if you can trace
A look of that smiling creature
Left now in my faded face.

It was like me once; but remember
The weary relentless years,
And Life, with its fierce, brief Tempests,
And its long, long rain of tears.

Is it strange to call it my Portrait?
Nay, smile, dear, for well you may,
To think of that radiant Vision
And of what I am to-day.

With restless, yet confident longing
How those blue eyes seem to gaze
Into deep and exhaustless Treasures,
All hid in the coming days.

With that trust which leans on the Future,
And counts on her promised store,
Until she has taught us to tremble
And hope,—but to trust no more.

How that young, light heart would have pitied
Me now—if her dreams had shown
A quiet and weary woman
With all her illusions flown.

Yet I—who shall soon be resting,
And have passed the hardest part,
Can look back with a deeper pity
On that young unconscious heart.

It is strange; but Life's currents drift us
So surely and swiftly on,
That we scarcely notice the changes,
And how many things are gone:

And forget, while to-day absorbs us,
How old mysteries are unsealed;
How the old, old ties are loosened,
And the old, old wounds are healed.

And we say that our Life is fleeting

Like a story that Time has told;
But we fancy that we—we only
Are just what we were of old.

So now and then it is wisdom
To gaze, as I do to-day,
At a half-forgotten relic
Of a Time that is passed away.

The very look of that Portrait,
The Perfume that seems to cling
To those fragile and faded letters,
And the Locket, and the Ring,

If they only stirred in my spirit
Forgotten pleasure and pain,—
Why, memory is often bitter,
And almost always in vain;

But the contrast of bygone hours
Comes to rend a veil away,—
And I marvel to see the stranger
Who is living in me to-day.

The Bride's Dream

The stars are gleaming;
The maiden sleeps—
What is she dreaming?
For see—she weeps.
By her side is an Angel
With folded wings;
While the Maiden slumbers
The Angel sings:
He sings of a Bridal,
Of Love, of Pain,
Of a heart to be given,—
And all in vain;
(See, her cheek is flushing,
As if with pain;)
He telleth of sorrow,
Regrets and fears,
And the few vain pleasures
We buy with tears;
And the bitter lesson
We learn from years.

The stars are gleaming
Upon her brow:
What is she dreaming
So calmly now?
By her side is the Angel
With folded wings;
She smiles in her slumber
The while he sings.
He sings of a Bridal,
Of Love divine;
Of a heart to be laid
On a sacred shrine;
Of a crown of glory,
Where seraphs shine;
Of the deep, long rapture
The chosen know
Who forsake for Heaven
Vain joys below,
Who desire no pleasure,
And fear no woe.

The Bells are ringing,
The sun shines clear,
The Choir is singing,
The guests are here.
Before the High Altar
Behold the Bride;
And a mournful Angel
Is by her side.
She smiles, all content
With her chosen lot,–
(Is her last night's dreaming
So soon forgot?)
And oh, may the Angel
Forsake her not!
For on her small hand
There glitters plain
The first sad link
Of a life-long chain;–
And she needs his guiding
Through paths of pain.

The Angel's Bidding

Not a sound is heard in the Convent;

The Vesper Chant is sung,
The sick have all been tended,
The poor nun's toils are ended
Till the Matin bell has rung.
All is still, save the Clock, that is ticking
So loud in the frosty air,
And the soft snow, falling as gently
As an answer to a prayer.
But an Angel whispers, "Oh, Sister,
You must rise from your bed to pray;
In the silent, deserted chapel,
You must kneel till the dawn of day;
For, far on the desolate moorland,
So dreary, and bleak, and white,
There is one, all alone and helpless,
In peril of death to-night.

"No sound on the moorland to guide him,
No star in the murky air;
And he thinks of his home and his loved ones
With the tenderness of despair;
He has wandered for hours in the snow-drift,
And he strives to stand in vain,
And so lies down to dream of his children
And never to rise again.
Then kneel in the silent chapel
Till the dawn of to-morrow's sun,
And ask of the Lord you worship
For the life of that desolate one;
And the smiling eyes of his children
Will gladden his heart again,
And the grateful tears of God's poor ones
Will fall on your soul like rain!—

"Yet, leave him alone to perish,
And the grace of your God implore,
With all the strength of your spirit,
For one who needs it more.
Far away, in the gleaming city,
Amid perfume, and song, and light,
A soul that Jesus has ransomed
Is in peril of sin to-night.

"The Tempter is close beside him,
And his danger is all forgot,
And the far-off voices of childhood
Call aloud, but he hears them not;
He sayeth no prayer, and his mother—

He thinks not of her to-day,
And he will not look up to Heaven,
And his Angel is turning away.

"Then pray for a soul in peril,
A soul for which Jesus died;
Ask, by the cross that bore Him,
And by her who stood beside;
And the Angels of God will thank you,
And bend from their thrones of light,
To tell you that Heaven rejoices
At the deed you have done to-night."

Evening Hymn

The shadows of the evening hours
Fall from the darkening sky;
Upon the fragrance of the flowers
The dews of evening lie:
Before Thy throne, O Lord of Heaven,
We kneel at close of day;
Look on Thy children from on high,
And hear us while we pray.

The sorrows of Thy Servants, Lord,
Oh, do not Thou despise;
But let the incense of our prayers
Before Thy mercy rise;
The brightness of the coming night
Upon the darkness rolls:
With hopes of future glory chase
The shadows on our souls.

Slowly the rays of daylight fade;
So fade within our heart,
The hopes in earthly love and joy,
That one by one depart:
Slowly the bright stars, one by one,
Within the Heavens shine;–
Give us, Oh, Lord, fresh hopes in Heaven,
And trust in things divine.

Let peace, Oh Lord, Thy peace, Oh God,
Upon our souls descend;
From midnight fears and perils, Thou
Our trembling hearts defend;

Give us a respite from our toil,
Calm and subdue our woes;
Through the long day we suffer, Lord,
Oh, give us now repose!

The Inner Chamber

In the outer Court I was singing,
Was singing the whole day long;
From the inner chamber were ringing
Echoes repeating my song.

And I sang till it grew immortal;
For that very song of mine,
When re-echoed behind the Portal,
Was filled with a life divine.

Was the Chamber a silver round
Of arches, whose magical art
Drew in coils of musical sound,
And cast them back on my heart?

Was there hidden within a lyre
Which, as air breathed over its strings,
Filled my song with a soul of fire,
And sent back my words with wings?

Was some seraph imprisoned there,
Whose voice made my song complete,
And whose lingering, soft despair,
Made the echo so faint and sweet?

Long I trembled and paused—then parted
The curtains with heavy fringe;
And, half fearing, yet eager-hearted
Turned the door on its golden hinge.

Now I sing in the court once more,
I sing and I weep all day,
As I kneel by the close-shut door,
For I know what the echoes say.

Yet I sing not the song of old,
Ere I knew whence the echo came,
Ere I opened the door of gold;
But the music sounds just the same.

Then take warning, and turn away
Do not ask of that hidden thing,
Do not guess what the echoes say,
Or the meaning of what I sing.

Hearts

I.

A trinket made like a Heart, dear,
Of red gold, bright and fine,
Was given to me for a keepsake,
Given to me for mine.

And another heart, warm and tender,
As true as a heart could be;
And every throb that stirred it
Was always and all for me.

Sailing over the waters,
Watching the far blue land,
I dropped my golden heart, dear,
Dropped it out of my hand!

It lies in the cold blue waters,
Fathoms and fathoms deep,
The golden heart which I promised,
Promised to prize and keep.

Gazing at Life's bright visions,
So false, and fair, and new,
I forgot the other heart, dear,
Forgot it and lost it too!

I might seek that heart for ever,
I might seek and seek in vain;—
And for one short, careless hour,
I pay with a life of pain.

II.

The Heart?—Yes I wore it
As sign and as token
Of a love that once gave it,
A vow that was spoken;
But a love, and a vow, and a heart

Can be broken.

The Love?—Life and Death
Are crushed into a day,
So what wonder that Love
Should as soon pass away—
What wonder I saw it
Fade, fail, and decay.

The Vow?—why what was it,
It snapped like a thread:
Who cares for the corpse
When the spirit is fled?
Then I said, "Let the Dead rise
And bury its dead,

"While the true, living future
Grows pure, wise, and strong"
So I cast the gold heart,
I had worn for so long,
In the Lake, and bound on it
A Stone—and a Wrong!

III.

Look, this little golden Heart
Was a true-love shrine
For a tress of hair; I held them,
Heart and tress, as mine,
Like the Love which gave the token
See to-day the Heart is broken!

Broken is the golden heart,
Lost the tress of hair;
Ah, the shrine is empty, vacant,
Desolate, and bare!
So the token should depart,
When Love dies within the heart.

Fast and deep the river floweth,
Floweth to the west;
I will cast the golden trinket
In its cold dark breast,—
Flow, oh river, deep and fast,
Over all the buried past!

Two Loves

Deep within my heart of hearts, dear,
Bound with all its strings,
Two Loves are together reigning
Both are crowned like Kings;
While my life, still uncomplaining,
Rests beneath their wings.

So they both will rule my heart, dear,
Till it cease to beat;
No sway can be deeper, stronger,
Truer, more complete;
Growing, as it lasts the longer,
Sweeter, and more sweet.

One all life and time transfigures,
Piercing through and through
Meaner things with magic splendour,
Old, yet ever new:
This,–so strong and yet so tender,–
Is . . . my Love for you.

Should it fail,–forgive my doubting
In this world of pain,–
Yet my other Love would ever
Steadfastly remain;
And I know that I could never
Turn to that in vain.

Though its radiance may be fainter,
Yet its task is wide;
For it lives to comfort sorrows,
Strengthen, calm, and guide,
And from Trust and Honour borrows
All its peace and pride.

Will you blame my dreaming even
If the first were flown?
Ah, I would not live without it,
It is all your own:
And the other–can you doubt it?–
Yours, and yours alone.

Past and Present

"Linger," I cried, "oh radiant Time! thy power

Has nothing more to give; life is complete:
Let but the perfect Present, hour by hour,
Itself remember and itself repeat.

"And Love,—the future can but mar its splendour,
Change can but dim the glory of its youth;
Time has no star more faithful or more tender,
To crown its constancy or light its truth."

But Time passed on in spite of prayer or pleading,
Through storm and peril; but that life might gain
A Peace through strife all other peace exceeding,
Fresh joy from sorrow, and new hope from pain.

And since Love lived when all save Love was dying,
And, passed through fire, grew stronger than before:-
Dear, you know why, in double faith relying,
I prize the Past much, but the Present more.

For the Future

I wonder did you ever count
The value of one human fate;
Or sum the infinite amount
Of one heart's treasures, and the weight
Of Life's one venture, and the whole concentrate purpose of a soul.

And if you ever paused to think
That all this in your hands I laid
Without a fear:- did you not shrink
From such a burthen? half afraid,
Half wishing that you could divide the risk, or cast it all aside.

While Love has daily perils, such
As none foresee and none control;
And hearts are strung so that one touch,
Careless or rough, may jar the whole,
You well might feel afraid to reign with absolute power of joy and pain.

You well might fear—if Love's sole claim
Were to be happy: but true Love
Takes joy as solace, not as aim,
And looks beyond, and looks above;
And sometimes through the bitterest strife first learns to live her
highest life.

Earth forges joy into a chain
Till fettered Love forgets its strength,
Its purpose, and its end;—but Pain
Restores its heritage at length,
And bids Love rise again and be eternal, mighty, pure, and free.

If then your future life should need
A strength my Love can only gain
Through suffering, or my heart be freed
Only by sorrow, from some stain—
Then you shall give, and I will take, this Crown of fire for Love's dear sake.

Sept. 8th, 1860.

Dream-Life

Listen, friend, and I will tell you
Why I sometimes seem so glad,
Then, without a reason changing,
Soon become so grave and sad.

Half my life I live a beggar,
Ragged, helpless, and alone;
But the other half a monarch,
With my courtiers round my throne.

Half my life is full of sorrow,
Half of joy, still fresh and new;
One of these lives is a fancy,
But the other one is true.

While I live and feast on gladness,
Still I feel the thought remain,
This must soon end,—nearer, nearer
Comes the life of grief and pain.

While I live a wretched beggar,
One bright hope my lot can cheer;
Soon, soon, thou shalt have thy kingdom,
Brighter hours are drawing near.

So you see my life is twofold,
Half a pleasure, half a grief;
Thus all joy is somewhat tempered,
And all sorrow finds relief.

Which, you ask me, is the real life,
Which the Dream—the joy, or woe?
Hush, friend! it is little matter,
And, indeed—I never know.

My Will

Since I have no lands or houses,
And no hoarded golden store,
What can I leave those who love me
When they see my face no more?
Do not smile; I am not jesting,
Though my words sound gay and light,
Listen to me, dearest Alice,
I will make my Will to-night.

First for Mabel—who will never
Let the dust of future years
Dim the thought of me, but keep it
Brighter still: perhaps with tears.
In whose eyes, whate'er I glance at,
Touch, or praise, will always shine,
Through a strange and sacred radiance,
By Love's Charter, wholly mine;
She will never lend to others
Slenderest link of thought I claim,
I will, therefore, to her keeping
Leave my memory and my name.

Bertha will do truer service
To her kind than I have done,
So I leave to her young spirit
The long Work I have begun.
Well! the threads are tangled, broken,
And the colours do not blend,
She will bend her earnest striving
Both to finish and amend:
And, when it is all completed,
Strong with care and rich with skill,
Just because my hands began it,
She will love it better still.

Ruth shall have my dearest token,
The one link I dread to break,
The one duty that I live for,
She, when I am gone, will take.

Sacred is the trust I leave her,
Needing patience, prayer, and tears;
I have striven to fulfil it,
As she knows—these many years.
Sometimes hopeless, faint, and weary
Yet a blessing shall remain
With the task, and Ruth will prize it
For my many hours of pain.

What must I leave you, my Alice?
Nothing, Love, to do or bear,
Nothing that can dim your blue eyes
With the slightest cloud of care.
I will leave my heart to love you,
With the tender faith of old;
Still to comfort, warm, and light you,
Should your life grow dark or cold.
No one else, my child, can claim it;
Though you find old scars of pain,
They were only wounds, my darling,
There is not, I trust, one stain.

Are my gifts indeed so worthless
Now the slender sum is told?
Well, I know not: years may bless them
With a nobler price than gold.
Am I poor? ah no, most wealthy,
Not in these poor gifts you take,
But in the true hearts that tell me
You will keep them for my sake.

King and Slave

If in my soul, dear,
An omen should dwell,
Bidding me pause, ere
I love thee too well;
If the whole circle,
Of noble and wise,
With stern forebodings,
Between us should rise.

I will tell them, dear,
That Love reigns—a King,
Where storms cannot reach him,
And words cannot sting;

He counts it dishonour
His faith to recall;
He trusts;—and for ever
He gives—and gives all!

I will tell thee, dear,
That Love is—a Slave,
Who dreads thought of freedom,
As life dreads the grave;
And if doubt or peril
Of change there may be,
Such fear would but drive him
Still nearer to thee!

A Chant

"Benedictus qui venit in nomine Domini."

I.

Who is the Angel that cometh?
Life!
Let us not question what he brings,
Peace or Strife,
Under the shade of his mighty wings,
One by one,
Are his secrets told;
One by one,
Lit by the rays of each morning sun,
Shall a new flower its petals unfold,
With the mystery hid in its heart of gold.
We will arise and go forth to greet him,
Singly, gladly, with one accord;—
"Blessed is he that cometh
In the name of the Lord!"

II.

Who is the Angel that cometh?
Joy!
Look at his glittering rainbow wings—
No alloy
Lies in the radiant gifts he brings;
Tender and sweet,
He is come to-day,
Tender and sweet:
While chains of love on his silver feet

Will hold him in lingering fond delay.
But greet him quickly, he will not stay,
Soon he will leave us; but though for others
All his brightest treasures are stored;—
"Blessed is he that cometh
In the name of the Lord!"

III.

Who is the Angel that cometh?
Pain!
Let us arise and go forth to greet him;
Not in vain
Is the summons come for us to meet him;
He will stay,
And darken our sun;
He will stay
A desolate night, a weary day.
Since in that shadow our work is done,
And in that shadow our crowns are won,
Let us say still, while his bitter chalice
Slowly into our hearts is poured,—
"Blessed is he that cometh
In the name of the Lord!"

IV.

Who is the Angel that cometh?
Death!
But do not shudder and do not fear;
Hold your breath,
For a kingly presence is drawing near.
Cold and bright
Is his flashing steel,
Cold and bright
The smile that comes like a starry light
To calm the terror and grief we feel;
He comes to help and to save and heal:
Then let us, baring our hearts and kneeling,
Sing, while we wait this Angel's sword,—
"Blessed is he that cometh
In the name of the Lord!"

Give Place

Starry Crowns of Heaven

Set in azure night!
Linger yet a little
Ere you hide your light:-
–Nay; let Starlight fade away
Heralding the day!

Snowflakes pure and spotless,
Still, oh, still remain,
Binding dreary winter,
In your silver chain:-
–Nay; but melt at once and bring
Radiant sunny Spring!

Blossoms, gentle blossoms,
Do not wither yet;
Still for you the sun shines,
Still the dews are wet:–
–Nay; but fade and wither last,
Fruit must come at last!

Joy, so true and tender,
Dare you not abide?
Will you spread your pinions,
Must you leave our side?
–Nay; an Angel's shining grace
Waits to fill your place!

A New Mother

I was with my lady when she died:
I it was who guided her weak hand
For a blessing on each little head,
Laid her baby by her on the bed,
Heard the words they could not understand.

And I drew them round my knee that night,
Hushed their childish glee, and made them say
They would keep her words with loving tears,
They would not forget her dying fears
Lest the thought of her should fade away.

I, who guessed what her last dread had been,
Made a promise to that still, cold face,
That her children's hearts, at any cost,
Should be with the mother they had lost,
When a stranger came to take her place.

And I knew so much! for I had lived
With my lady since her childhood: known
What her young and happy days had been,
And the grief no other eyes had seen
I had watched and sorrowed for alone.

Ah! she once had such a happy smile!
I had known how sorely she was tried:
Six short years before, her eyes were bright
As her little blue-eyed May's that night,
When she stood by her dead mother's side.

No—I will not say he was unkind;
But she had been used to love and praise.
He was somewhat grave—perhaps, in truth,
Could not weave her joyous, smiling youth,
Into all his stern and serious ways.

She, who should have reigned a blooming flower,
First in pride and honour, as in grace,—
She, whose will had once ruled all around,
Queen and darling of us all—she found
Change indeed in that cold, stately place.

Yet she would not blame him, even to me,
Though she often sat and wept alone;
But she could not hide it near her death,
When she said with her last struggling breath,
"Let my babies still remain my own!"

I it was who drew the sheet aside,
When he saw his dead wife's face. That test
Seemed to strike right to his heart. He said,
In a strange, low whisper, to the dead,
"God knows, love, I did it for the best!"

And he wept—Oh yes, I will be just—
When I brought the children to him there—
Wondering sorrow in their baby eyes;
And he soothed them with his fond replies,
Bidding me give double love and care.

Ah, I loved them well for her dear sake:
Little Arthur, with his serious air;
May, with all her mother's pretty ways,
Blushing, and at any word of praise
Shaking out her sunny golden hair.

And the little one of all–poor child!
She had cost that dear and precious life.
Once Sir Arthur spoke my lady's name,
When the baby's gloomy christening came,
And he called her "Olga–like my wife!"

Save that time, he never spoke of her;
He grew graver, sterner, every day;
And the children felt it, for they dropped
Low their voices, and their laughter stopped
While he stood and watched them at their play.

No, he never named their mother's name.
But I told them of her: told them all
She had been; so gentle, good, and bright;
And I always took them every night
Where her picture hung in the great hall.

There she stood: white daisies in her hand,
And her red lips parted as to speak
With a smile; the blue and sunny air
Seemed to stir her floating golden hair,
And to bring a faint blush on her cheek.

Well, so time passed on; a year was gone,
And Sir Arthur had been much away.
Then the news came! I shed many tears
When I saw the truth of all my fears
Rise before me on that bitter day.

Any one but her I could have borne!
But my lady loved her as her friend.
Through their childhood and their early youth,
How she used to count upon the truth
Of this friendship that would never end!

Older, graver than my lady was,
Whose young, gentle heart on her relied,
She would give advice, and praise, and blame,
And my lady leant on Margaret's name,
As her dearest comfort, help, and guide.

I had never liked her, and I think
That my lady grew to doubt her too,
Since her marriage; for she named her less,
Never saw her, and I used to guess
At some secret wrong I never knew.

That might be or not. But now, to hear
She would come and reign here in her stead,
With the pomp and splendour of a bride:
Would no thought reproach her in her pride
With the silent memory of the dead?

So, the day came, and the bells rang out,
And I laid the children's black aside;
And I held each little trembling hand,
As I strove to make them understand
They must greet their father's new-made bride.

Ah, Sir Arthur might look grave and stern,
And his lady's eyes might well grow dim,
When the children shrank in fear away,—
Little Arthur hid his face, and May
Would not raise her eyes, or speak to him.

When Sir Arthur bade them greet their "mother,"
I was forced to chide, yet proud to hear
How my little loving May replied,
With her mother's pretty air of pride,—
"Our dear mother has been dead a year!"

Ah, the lady's tears might well fall fast,
As she kissed them, and then turned away.
She might strive to smile or to forget,
But I think some shadow of regret
Must have risen to blight her wedding-day.

She had some strange touch of self-reproach;
For she used to linger day by day,
By the nursery door, or garden gate,
With a sad, calm, wistful look, and wait
Watching the three children at their play.

But they always shrank away from her
When she strove to comfort their alarms,
And their grave, cold silence to beguile:
Even little Olga's baby-smile
Quivered into tears when in her arms.

I could never chide them: for I saw
How their mother's memory grew more deep
In their hearts. Each night I had to tell
Stories of her whom I loved so well
When a child, to send them off to sleep.

But Sir Arthur–Oh, this was too hard!–
He, who had been always stern and sad
In my lady's time, seemed to rejoice
Each day more; and I could hear his voice
Even, sounding younger and more glad.

He might perhaps have blamed them, but his wife
Never failed to take the children's part:
She would stay him with her pleading tone,
Saying she would strive, and strive alone,
Till she gained each little wayward heart.

And she strove indeed, and seemed to be
Always waiting for their love, in vain;
Yet, when May had most her mother's look,
Then the lady's calm, cold accents shook
With some memory of reproachful pain.

Little May would never call her Mother:
So, one day, the lady, bending low,
Kissed her golden curls, and softly said,
"Sweet one, call me Margaret, instead,–
Your dear mother used to call me so."

She was gentle, kind, and patient too,
Yet in vain: the children held apart.
Ah, their mother's gentle memory dwelt
Near them, and her little orphans felt
She had the first claim upon their heart.

So three years passed; then the war broke out;
And a rumour seemed to spread and rise;
First we guessed what sorrow must befall,
Then all doubt fled, for we read it all
In the depths of her despairing eyes.

Yes; Sir Arthur had been called away
To that scene of slaughter, fear, and strife,–
Now he seemed to know with double pain,
The cold, bitter gulf that must remain
To divide his children from his wife.

Nearer came the day he was to sail,
Deeper grew the coming woe and fear,
When, one night, the children at my knee
Knelt to say their evening prayer to me,
I looked up and saw Sir Arthur near.

There they knelt with folded hands, and said
Low, soft words in stammering accents sweet;
In the firelight shone their golden hair
And white robes: my darlings looked so fair,
With their little bare and rosy feet!

There he waited till their low "Amen;"
Stopped the rosy lips raised for "Good night!"—
Drew them with a fond clasp, close and near,
As he bade them stay with him, and hear
Something that would make his heart more light.

Little Olga crept into his arms;
Arthur leant upon his shoulder; May
Knelt beside him, with her earnest eyes
Lifted up in patient, calm surprise—
I can almost hear his words to-day.

"Years ago, my children, years ago,
When your mother was a child, she came
From her northern home, and here she met
Love for love, and comfort for regret,
In one early friend,—you know her name.

"And this friend—a few years older—gave
Such fond care, such love, that day by day
The new home grew happy, joy complete,
Studies easier, and play more sweet,
While all childish sorrows passed away.

"And your mother—fragile, like my May—
Leant on this deep love,—nor leant in vain.
For this friend (strong, generous, noble heart!)
Gave the sweet, and took the bitter part,—
Brought her all the joy, and kept the pain.

"Years passed on, and then I saw them first:
It was hard to say which was most fair,
Your sweet mother's bright and blushing face,
Or the graver Margaret's stately grace;
Golden locks, or braided raven hair.

"Then it happened, by a strange, sad fate,
One thought entered into each young soul:
Joy for one—if for the other pain;
Loss for one—if for the other gain:
One must lose, and one possess the whole.

"And so this—this—what they cared for—came
And belonged to Margaret: was her own.
But she laid the gift aside, to take
Pain and sorrow for your mother's sake,
And none knew it but herself alone.

"Then she travelled far away, and none
The strange mystery of her absence knew.
Margaret's secret thought was never told:
Even your mother thought her changed and cold,
And for many years I thought so too.

"She was gone; and then your mother took
That poor gift which Margaret laid aside:
Flower, or toy, or trinket, matters not:
What it was had better be forgot . . .
It was just then she became my bride.

"Now, I think May knows the hope I have.
Arthur, darling, can you guess the rest?
Even my little Olga understands
Great gifts can be given by little hands,
Since of all gifts Love is still the best.

"Margaret is my dear and honoured wife,
And I hold her so. But she can claim
From your hearts, dear ones, a loving debt
I can neither pay, nor yet forget:
You can give it in your mother's name.

"Earth spoils even Love, and here a shade
On the purest, noblest heart may fall:
Now your mother dwells in perfect light,
She will bless us, I believe, to-night,—
She is happy now, and she knows all."

Next day was farewell—a day of tears;
Yet Sir Arthur, as he rode away,
And turned back to see his lady stand
With the children clinging to her hand,
Looked as if it were a happy day.

Ah, they loved her soon! The little one
Crept into her arms as to a nest;
Arthur always with her now; and May
Growing nearer to her every day:—
—Well, I loved my own dear lady best.

A Lost Chord

Seated one day at the Organ,
I was weary and ill at ease,
And my fingers wandered idly
Over the noisy keys.

I do not know what I was playing,
Or what I was dreaming then;
But I struck one chord of music,
Like the sound of a great Amen.

It flooded the crimson twilight
Like the close of an Angel's Psalm,
And it lay on my fevered spirit
With a touch of infinite calm.

It quieted pain and sorrow,
Like love overcoming strife;
It seemed the harmonious echo
From our discordant life.

It linked all perplexed meanings
Into one perfect peace,
And trembled away into silence
As if it were loth to cease.

I have sought, but I seek it vainly,
That one lost chord divine,
Which came from the soul of the Organ,
And entered into mine.

It may be that Death's bright angel
Will speak in that chord again,—
It may be that only in Heaven
I shall hear that grand Amen.

True or False

So you think you love me, do you?
Well, it may be so;
But there are many ways of loving
I have learnt to know.
Many ways, and but one true way,

Which is very rare;
And the counterfeits look brightest,
Though they will not wear.

Yet they ring, almost, quite truly,
Last (with care) for long;
But in time must break, may shiver
At a touch of wrong:
Having seen what looked most real
Crumble into dust;
Now I chose that test and trial
Should precede my trust.

I have seen a love demanding
Time and hope and tears,
Chaining all the past, exacting
Bonds from future years;
Mind and heart, and joy and sorrow,
Claiming as its fee:
That was Love of Self, and never,
Never Love of me!

I have seen a love forgetting
All above, beyond,
Linking every dream and fancy
In a sweeter bond;
Counting every hour worthless,
Which was cold or free:-
That, perhaps, was—Love of Pleasure,
But not Love of me!

I have seen a love whose patience
Never turned aside,
Full of tender, fond devices;
Constant, even when tried;
Smallest boons were held as victories,
Drops that swelled the sea:
That I think was—Love of Power,
But not Love of me!

I have seen a love disdaining
Ease and pride and fame,
Burning even its own white pinions
Just to feed its flame;
Reigning thus, supreme, triumphant,
By the soul's decree;
That was—Love of Love, I fancy,
But not Love of me!

I have heard—or dreamt, it may be—
What Love is when true;
How to test and how to try it,
Is the gift of few:
These few say (or did I dream it?)
That true Love abides
In these very things, but always
Has a soul besides.

Lives among the false loves, knowing
Just their peace and strife:
Bears the self-same look, but always
Has an inner life.
Only a true heart can find it,
True as it is true,
Only eyes as clear and tender
Look it through and through.

If it dies, it will not perish
By Time's slow decay,
True Love only grows (they tell me)
Stronger, day by day:
Pain—has been its friend and comrade;
Fate—it can defy;
Only by its own sword, sometimes
Love can choose to die.

And its grave shall be more noble
And more sacred still,
Than a throne, where one less worthy
Reigns and rules at will.
Tell me then, do you dare offer
This true Love to me? . . .
Neither you nor I can answer;
We will—wait and see!

Over the Mountain

Like dreary prison walls
The stern grey mountains rise,
Until their topmost crags
Touch the far gloomy skies:
One steep and narrow path
Winds up the mountain's crest,
And from our valley leads
Out to the golden West.

I dwell here in content,
Thankful for tranquil days;
And yet, my eyes grow dim,
As still I gaze and gaze
Upon that mountain pass,
That leads—or so it seems—
To some far happy land,
Known in a world of dreams.

And as I watch that path
Over the distant hill,
A foolish longing comes
My heart and soul to fill,
A painful, strange desire
To break some weary bond,
A vague unuttered wish
For what might lie beyond!

In that far world unknown,
Over that distant hill,
May dwell the loved and lost,
Lost—yet beloved still;
I have a yearning hope,
Half longing, and half pain,
That by that mountain pass
They may return again.

Space may keep friends apart,
Death has a mighty thrall;
There is another gulf
Harder to cross than all;
Yet watching that far road,
My heart beats full and fast—
If they should come once more,
If they should come at last!

See, down the mountain side
The silver vapours creep;
They hide the rocky cliffs.
They hide the craggy steep,
They hide the narrow path
That comes across the hill—
Oh, foolish longing, cease,
Oh, beating Heart, be still!

Envy

He was the first always: Fortune
Shone bright in his face.
I fought for years; with no effort
He conquered the place:
We ran; my feet were all bleeding,
But he won the race.

Spite of his many successes
Men loved him the same;
My one pale ray of good fortune
Met scoffing and blame.
When we erred, they gave him pity,
But me—only shame.

My home was still in the shadow,
His lay in the sun:
I longed in vain: what he asked for
It straightway was done.
Once I staked all my heart's treasure,
We played—and he won.

Yes; and just now I have seen him,
Cold, smiling, and blest,
Laid in his coffin. God help me!
While he is at rest,
I am cursed still to live:- even
Death loved him the best.

A Legend of Provence

The lights extinguished, by the hearth I leant,
Half weary with a listless discontent.
The flickering giant-shadows, gathering near,
Closed round me with a dim and silent fear.
All dull, all dark; save when the leaping flame,
Glancing, lit up a Picture's ancient frame.
Above the hearth it hung. Perhaps the night,
My foolish tremors, or the gleaming light,
Lent power to that Portrait dark and quaint—
A Portrait such as Rembrandt loved to paint—
The likeness of a Nun. I seemed to trace
A world of sorrow in the patient face,
In the thin hands folded across her breast—
Its own and the room's shadow hid the rest.
I gazed and dreamed, and the dull embers stirred,
Till an old legend that I once had heard

Came back to me; linked to the mystic gloom
Of that dark Picture in the ghostly room.
In the far south, where clustering vines are hung;
Where first the old chivalric lays were sung,
Where earliest smiled that gracious child of France,
Angel and knight and fairy, called Romance,
I stood one day. The warm blue June was spread
Upon the earth; blue summer overhead,
Without a cloud to fleck its radiant glare,
Without a breath to stir its sultry air.
All still, all silent, save the sobbing rush
Of rippling waves, that lapsed in silver hush
Upon the beach; where, glittering towards the strand,
The purple Mediterranean kissed the land.

All still, all peaceful; when a convent chime
Broke on the mid-day silence for a time,
Then trembling into quiet, seemed to cease,
In deeper silence and more utter peace.
So as I turned to gaze, where gleaming white,
Half hid by shadowy trees from passers' sight,
The Convent lay, one who had dwelt for long
In that fair home of ancient tale and song,
Who knew the story of each cave and hill,
And every haunting fancy lingering still
Within the land, spake thus to me, and told
The Convent's treasured Legend, quaint and old:

Long years ago, a dense and flowering wood,
Still more concealed where the white convent stood,
Borne on its perfumed wings the title came:
"Our Lady of the Hawthorns" is its name.
Then did that bell, which still rings out to-day,
Bid all the country rise, or eat, or pray.
Before that convent shrine, the haughty knight
Passed the lone vigil of his perilous fight;
For humbler cottage strife or village brawl,
The Abbess listened, prayed, and settled all.
Young hearts that came, weighed down by love or wrong,
Left her kind presence comforted and strong.
Each passing pilgrim, and each beggar's right
Was food, and rest, and shelter for the night.
But, more than this, the Nuns could well impart
The deepest mysteries of the healing art;
Their store of herbs and simples was renowned,
And held in wondering faith for miles around.
Thus strife, love, sorrow, good and evil fate,
Found help and blessing at the convent gate.

Of all the nuns, no heart was half so light,
No eyelids veiling glances half as bright,
No step that glided with such noiseless feet,
No face that looked so tender or so sweet,
No voice that rose in choir so pure, so clear,
No heart to all the others half so dear,
So surely touched by others' pain or woe,
(Guessing the grief her young life could not know,)
No soul in childlike faith so undefiled,
As Sister Angela's, the "Convent Child."
For thus they loved to call her. She had known
No home, no love, no kindred, save their own.
An orphan, to their tender nursing given,
Child, plaything, pupil, now the Bride of Heaven.
And she it was who trimmed the lamp's red light
That swung before the altar, day and night;
Her hands it was whose patient skill could trace
The finest broidery, weave the costliest lace;
But most of all, her first and dearest care,
The office she would never miss or share,
Was every day to weave fresh garlands sweet,
To place before the shrine at Mary's feet.
Nature is bounteous in that region fair,
For even winter has her blossoms there.
Thus Angela loved to count each feast the best,
By telling with what flowers the shrine was dressed.
In pomp supreme the countless Roses passed,
Battalion on battalion thronging fast,
Each with a different banner, flaming bright,
Damask, or striped, or crimson, pink, or white,
Until they bowed before a newborn queen,
And the pure virgin Lily rose serene.
Though Angela always thought the Mother blest
Must love the time of her own hawthorn best,
Each evening through the year, with equal, care,
She placed her flowers; then kneeling down in prayer,
As their faint perfume rose before the shrine,
So rose her thoughts, as pure and as divine.
She knelt until the shades grew dim without,
Till one by one the altar lights shone out,
Till one by one the Nuns, like shadows dim,
Gathered around to chant their vesper hymn;
Her voice then led the music's winged flight,
And "Ave, Maris Stella" filled the night.
But wherefore linger on those days of peace?
When storms draw near, then quiet hours must cease.
War, cruel war, defaced the land, and came

So near the convent with its breath of flame,
That, seeking shelter, frightened peasants fled,
Sobbing out tales of coming fear and dread,
Till after a fierce skirmish, down the road,
One night came straggling soldiers, with their load
Of wounded, dying comrades; and the band,
Half pleading yet as if they could command,
Summoned the trembling Sisters, craved their care,
Then rode away, and left the wounded there.
But soon compassion bade all fear depart.
And bidding every Sister do her part,
Some prepare simples, healing salves, or bands,
The Abbess chose the more experienced hands,
To dress the wounds needing most skilful care;
Yet even the youngest Novice took her share.
To Angela, who had but ready will
And tender pity, yet no special skill,
Was given the charge of a young foreign knight,
Whose wounds were painful, but whose danger slight.
Day after day she watched beside his bed,
And first in hushed repose the hours fled:
His feverish moans alone the silence stirred,
Or her soft voice, uttering some pious word.
At last the fever left him; day by day
The hours, no longer silent, passed away.
What could she speak of? First, to still his plaints,
She told him legends of the martyred Saints;
Described the pangs, which, through God's plenteous grace,
Had gained their souls so high and bright a place.
This pious artifice soon found success—
Or so she fancied—for he murmured less.
So she described the glorious pomp sublime,
In which the chapel shone at Easter time,
The Banners, Vestments, gold, and colours bright,
Counted how many tapers gave their light;
Then, in minute detail went on to say,
How the High Altar looked on Christmas-day:
The kings and shepherds, all in green and red,
And a bright star of jewels overhead.
Then told the sign by which they all had seen,
How even nature loved to greet her Queen,
For, when Our Lady's last procession went
Down the long garden, every head was bent,
And, rosary in hand, each Sister prayed;
As the long floating banners were displayed,
They struck the hawthorn boughs, and showers and showers
Of buds and blossoms strewed her way with flowers.
The Knight unwearied listened; till at last,

He too described the glories of his past;
Tourney, and joust, and pageant bright and fair,
And all the lovely ladies who were there.
But half incredulous she heard. Could this—
This be the world? this place of love and bliss!
Where then was hid the strange and hideous charm,
That never failed to bring the gazer harm?
She crossed herself, yet asked, and listened still,
And still the knight described with all his skill
The glorious world of joy, all joys above,
Transfigured in the golden mist of love.
Spread, spread your wings, ye angel guardians bright,
And shield these dazzling phantoms from her sight!
But no; days passed, matins and vespers rang,
And still the quiet Nuns toiled, prayed, and sang,
And never guessed the fatal, coiling net
Which every day drew near, and nearer yet,
Around their darling; for she went and came
About her duties, outwardly the same.
The same? ah, no! even when she knelt to pray,
Some charmed dream kept all her heart away.
So days went on, until the convent gate
Opened one night. Who durst go forth so late?
Across the moonlit grass, with stealthy tread,
Two silent, shrouded figures passed and fled.
And all was silent, save the moaning seas,
That sobbed and pleaded, and a wailing breeze
That sighed among the perfumed hawthorn trees.

Optimus

There is a deep and subtle snare
Whose sure temptation hardly fails,
Which, just because it looks so fair,
Only a noble heart assails.

So all the more we need be strong
Against this false and seeming Right;
Which none the less is deadly wrong,
Because it glitters clothed in light.

When duties unfulfilled remain,
Or noble works are left unplanned,
Or when great deeds cry out in vain
On coward heart and trembling hand,—

Then will a seeming Angel speak:–
"The hours are fleeting–great the need–
If thou art strong and others weak,
Thine be the effort and the deed.

"Deaf are their ears who ought to hear;
Idle their hands, and dull their soul;
While sloth, or ignorance, or fear,
Fetters them with a blind control.

"Sort thou the tangled web aright;
Take thou the toil–take thou the pain:
For fear the hour begin its flight,
While Right and Duty plead in vain."

And now it is I bid thee pause,
Nor let this Tempter bend thy will:
There are diviner, truer laws
That teach a nobler lesson still.

Learn that each duty makes its claim
Upon one soul: not each on all.
How, if God speaks thy Brother's name,
Dare thou make answer to the call?

The greater peril in the strife,
The less this evil should be done;
For as in battle, so in life,
Danger and honour still are one.

Arouse him then:- this is thy part:
Show him the claim; point out the need;
And nerve his arm, and cheer his heart;
Then stand aside, and say "God speed!"

Smooth thou his path ere it is trod;
Burnish the arms that he must wield;
And pray, with all thy strength, that God
May crown him Victor of the field.

And then, I think, thy soul shall feel
A nobler thrill of true content,
Than if presumptuous, eager zeal
Had seized a crown for others meant.

And even that very deed shall shine
In mystic sense, divine and true,
More wholly and more purely thine–

Because it is another's too.

Many, if God should make them kings,
Might not disgrace the throne He gave;
How few who could as well fulfil
The holier office of a slave.

I hold him great who, for Love's sake
Can give, with generous, earnest will,–
Yet he who takes for Love's sweet sake,
I think I hold more generous still.

I prize the instinct that can turn
From vain pretence with proud disdain;
Yet more I prize a simple heart;
Paying credulity with pain.

I bow before the noble mind
That freely some great wrong forgives;
Yet nobler is the one forgiven,
Who bears that burden well, and lives.

It may be hard to gain, and still
To keep a lowly steadfast heart
Yet he who loses has to fill
A harder and a truer part.

Glorious it is to wear the crown
Of a deserved and pure success;–
He who knows how to fail has won
A Crown whose lustre is not less.

Great may he be who can command
And rule with just and tender sway;
Yet is diviner wisdom taught
Better by him who can obey.

Blessed are those who die for God,
And earn the Martyr's crown of light–
Yet he who lives for God may be
A greater Conqueror in His sight.

Yes, I was sad and anxious,
But now, dear, I am gay;
I know that it is wisest
To put all hope away:-
Thank God that I have done so
And can be calm to-day.

For hope deferred—you know it,
Once made my heart so sick:
Now, I expect no longer;
It is but the old trick
Of hope, that makes me tremble,
And makes my heart beat quick.

All day I sit here calmly;
Not as I did before,
Watching for one whose footstep
Comes never, never more . . .
Hush! was that someone passing,
Who paused beside the door?

For years I hung on chances,
Longing for just one word;
At last I feel it:- silence
Will never more be stirred . . .
Tell me once more that rumour,
You fancied you had heard.

Life has more things to dwell on
Than just one useless pain,
Useless and past for ever;
But noble things remain,
And wait us all: . . . you too, dear,
Do you think hope quite vain?

All others have forgotten,
'Tis right I should forget,
Nor live on a keen longing
Which shadows forth regret: . . .
Are not the letters coming?
The sun is almost set.

Now that my restless legion
Of hopes and fears is fled,
Reading is joy and comfort . . .
. . . This very day I read,

Oh, such a strange returning
Of one whom all thought dead!

Not that I dream or fancy,
You know all that is past;
Earth has no hope to give me,
And yet:- Time flies so fast
That all but the impossible
Might be brought back at last.

The Requital

Loud roared the Tempest,
Fast fell the sleet;
A little Child Angel
Passed down the street,
With trailing pinions,
And weary feet.

The moon was hidden;
No stars were bright;
So she could not shelter
In heaven that night,
For the Angels' ladders
Are rays of light.

She beat her wings
At each window pane,
And pleaded for shelter,
But all in vain:–
"Listen," they said,
"To the pelting rain!"

She sobbed, as the laughter
And mirth grew higher,
"Give me rest and shelter
Beside your fire,
And I will give you
Your heart's desire."

The dreamer sat watching
His embers gleam,
While his heart was floating
Down hope's bright stream;
. . . So he wove her wailing
Into his dream.

The worker toiled on,
For his time was brief;
The mourner was nursing
Her own pale grief:
They heard not the promise
That brought relief.

But fiercer the Tempest
Rose than before,
When the Angel paused
At a humble door,
And asked for shelter
And help once more.

A weary woman,
Pale, worn, and thin,
With the brand upon her
Of want and sin,
Heard the Child Angel
And took her in.

Took her in gently,
And did her best
To dry her pinions;
And made her rest
With tender pity
Upon her breast.

When the eastern morning
Grew bright and red,
Up the first sunbeam
The Angel fled;
Having kissed the woman
And left her—dead.

A False Genius

I see a Spirit by thy side,
Purple-winged and eagle-eyed,
Looking like a Heavenly guide.

Though he seem so bright and fair,
Ere thou trust his proffered care,
Pause a little, and beware!

If he bid thee dwell apart,
Tending some ideal smart

In a sick and coward heart;

In self-worship wrapped alone,
Dreaming thy poor griefs are grown
More than other men have known;

Dwelling in some cloudy sphere,
Though God's work is waiting here,
And God deigneth to be near;

If his torch's crimson glare
Show thee evil everywhere,
Tainting all the wholesome air;

While with strange distorted choice,
Still disdaining to rejoice,
Thou wilt hear a wailing voice;

If a simple, humble heart,
Seem to thee a meaner part,
Than thy noblest aim and art;

If he bid thee bow before
Crowned Mind and nothing more,
The great idol men adore;

And with starry veil enfold
Sin, the trailing serpent old,
Till his scales shine out like gold;

Though his words seem true and wise,
Soul, I say to thee—Arise.
He is a Demon in disguise!

The Ghost in the Picture Room

Published as part of The Haunted House, a collection including Charles Dickens and Wilkie Collins

Belinda, with a modest self-possession quite her own, promptly answered for this Spectre in a low, clear voice:

The lights extinguished; by the hearth I leant,
Half weary with a listless discontent.
The flickering giant shadows, gathering near.
Closed round me with a dim and silent fear;

All dull, all dark; save when the leaping flame,
Glancing, lit up The Picture's ancient frame.
Above the hearth it hung. Perhaps the night,
My foolish tremors, or the gleaming light,
Lent Power to that Portrait dark and quaint —
A Portrait such as Rembrandt loved to paint —
The likeness of a Nun. I seemed to trace
A world of sorrow in the patient face,
In the thin hands folded across her breast —
Its own and the room's shadow hid the rest.
I gazed and dreamed, and the dull embers stirred,
Till an old legend that I once had heard
Came back to me; linked to the mystic gloom
Of the dark Picture in the ghostly room.

In the far South, where clustering vines are hung;
Where first the old chivalric lays were sung;
Where earliest smiled that gracious child of France,
Angel and Knight and Fairy, called Romance,
I stood one day. The warm blue June was spread
Upon the earth; blue summer overhead,
Without a cloud to fleck its radiant glare,
Without a breath to stir its sultry air.
All still, all silent, save the sobbing rush
Of rippling waves, that lapsed in silver hush
Upon the beach; where, glittering towards the strand,
The purple Mediterranean kissed the land.

All still, all peaceful; when a convent chime
Broke on the midday silence for a time,
Then trembling into quiet, seemed to cease,
In deeper silence and more utter peace.
So as I turned to gaze, where gleaming white,
Half hid by shadowy trees from passers' sight,
The convent lay, one who had dwelt for long
In that fair home of ancient tale and song,
Who knew the story of each cave and hill,
And every haunting fancy lingering still
Within the land, spake thus to me, and told
The convent's treasured legend, quaint and old:

Long years ago, a dense and flowering wood,
Still more concealed where the white convent stood,
Borne on its perfumed wings the title came:
"Our Lady of the Hawthorns" is its name.
Then did that bell, which still rings out today
Bid all the country rise, or eat, or pray.
Before that convent shrine, the haughty knight

Passed the lone vigil of his perilous fight;
For humbler cottage strife, or village brawl,
The abbess listened, prayed, and settled all.
Young hearts that came, weighed down by love or wrong,

Left her kind presence comforted and strong.
Each passing pilgrim, and each beggar's right
Was food, and rest, and shelter for the night.
But, more than this, the nuns could well impart
The deepest mysteries of the healing art;
Their store of herbs and simples was renowned,
And held in wondering faith for miles around.
Thus strife, love, sorrow, good and evil fate,
Found help and blessing at the convent gate.

Of all the nuns, no heart was half so light,
No eyelids veiling glances half as bright,
No step that glided with such noiseless feet,
No face that looked so tender or so sweet,
No voice that rose in choir so pure, so clear,
No heart to all the others half so dear
(So surely touched by others' pain or woe,
Guessing the grief her young life could not know),
No soul in childlike faith so undefiled,
As Sister Angela's, the "Convent Child."
For thus they loved to call her. She had known
No home, no love, no kindred, save their own —
An orphan, to their tender nursing given,
Child, plaything, pupil, now the bride of Heaven.
And she it was who trimmed the lamp's red light
That swung before the altar, day and night.
Her hands it was, whose patient skill could trace
The finest broidery, weave the costliest lace;
But most of all, her first and dearest care,
The office she would never miss or share,
Was every day to weave fresh garlands sweet,
To place before the shrine at Mary's feet.
Nature is bounteous in that region fair,
For even winter has her blossoms there.
Thus Angela loved to count each feast the best,
By telling with what flowers the shrine was dressed.
In pomp supreme the countless Roses passed,
Battalion on battalion thronging fast,
Each with a different banner, flaming bright,
Damask, or striped, or crimson, pink, or white,
Until they bowed before the new-born queen,
And the pure virgin lily rose serene.
Though Angela always thought the Mother blest,

Must love the time of her own hawthorns best
Each evening through the year, with equal care,
She placed her flowers; then kneeling down in prayer,
As their faint perfume rose before the shrine,
So rose her thoughts, as pure and as divine.
She knelt until the shades grew dim without,
Till one by one the altar lights shone out,
Till one by one the nuns, like shadows dim,
Gathered around to chant their vesper hymn:
Her voice then led the music's winged flight,
And "Ave, Maris Stella" filled the night.

But wherefore linger on those days of peace?
When storms draw near, then quiet hours must cease.
War, cruel war, defaced the land, and came
So near the convent with its breath of flame,
That, seeking shelter, frightened peasants fled,
Sobbing out tales of coming fear and dread.
Till after a fierce skirmish, down the road,
One night came straggling soldiers, with their load
Of wounded, dying comrades; and the band,
Half pleading, yet as if they could command,
Summoned the trembling sisters, craved their care,
Then rode away, and left the wounded there.
But soon compassion bade all fear depart,
And bidding every sister do her part,
Some prepare simples, healing salves, or bands,
The abbess chose the more experienced hands,
To dress the wounds needing most skilful care;
Yet even the youngest novice took her share,
And thus to Angela, whose ready will
And pity could not cover lack of skill,
The charge of a young wounded knight must fall,
A case which seemed least dangerous of them all.
Day after day she watched beside his bed,
And first in utter quiet the hours fled:
His feverish moans alone the silence stirred,
Or her soft voice, uttering some pious word.
At last the fever left him; day by day
The hours, no longer silent, passed away.
What could she speak of? First, to still his plaint,
She told him legends of the martyr'd saints;
Described the pangs, which, through God's plenteous grace,
Had gained their souls so high and bright a place.
This pious artifice soon found success
Or so she fancied for he murmured less.
And so she told the pomp and grand array
In which the chapel shone on Easter Day,

Described the vestments, gold, and colours bright,
Counted how many tapers gave their light;
Then, in minute detail went on to say,
How the high altar looked on Christmas day:
The kings and shepherds, all in green and white,
And a large star of jewels gleaming bright.
Then told the sign by which they all had seen,
How even nature loved to greet her Queen,
For, when Our Lady's last procession went
Down the long garden, every head was bent,
And rosary in hand each sister prayed;
As the long floating banners were displayed,
They struck the hawthorn boughs, and showers and showers
Of buds and blossoms strewed her way with flowers.
The knight unwearied listened; till at last,
He too described the glories of his past;
Tourney, and joust, and pageant bright and fair,
And all the lovely ladies who were there.
But half incredulous she heard. Could this
This be the world? this place of love and bliss!
Where, then, was hid tha strange and hideous charm,
That never failed to bring the gazer harm?
She crossed herself, yet asked, and listened still,
And still the knight described with all his skill,
The glorious world of joy, all joys above,
Transfigured in the golden mist of love.
Spread, spread your wings, ye angel guardians bright,
And shield these dazzling phantoms from her sight!
But no; days passed, matins and vespers rang,
And still the quiet nuns toiled, prayed, and sang,
And never guessed the fatal, coiling net
That every day drew near, and nearer yet.
Around their darling; for she went and came
About her duties, outwardly the same.
The same? ah, no! even when she knelt to pray,
Some charmed dream kept all her heart away.
So days went on, until the convent gate
Opened one night. Who durst go forth so late?
Across the moonlit grass, with stealthy tread,
Two silent, shrouded figures passed and fled.
And all was silent, save the moaning seas,
That sobbed and pleaded, and a wailing breeze
That sighed among the perfumed hawthorn trees.

What need to tell that dream so bright and brief,
Of joy unchequered by a dread of grief?
What need to tell how all such dreams must fade,
Before the slow foreboding, dreaded shade,

That floated nearer, until pomp and pride,
Pleasure and wealth, were summoned to her side,
To bid, at least, the noisy hours forget,
And clamour down the whispers of regret.
Still Angela strove to dream, and strove in vain;
Awakened once, she could not sleep again.
She saw, each day and hour, more worthless grown
The heart for which she cast away her own;
And her soul learnt, through bitterest inward strife,
The slight, frail love for which she wrecked her life;
The phantom for which all her hope was given,
The cold bleak earth for which she bartered heaven!
But all in vain; what chance remained? what heart
Would stoop to take so poor an outcast's part?
Years fled, and she grew reckless more and more,
Until the humblest peasant closed his door,
And where she passed, fair dames, in scorn and pride,
Shuddered, and drew their rustling robes aside.
At last a yearning seemed to fill her soul,
A longing that was stronger than control:
Once more, just once again, to see the place
That knew her young and innocent; to retrace
The long and weary southern path; to gaze
Upon the haven of her childish days;
Once more beneath the convent roof to lie;
Once more to look upon her home — and die!
Weary and worn — her comrades, chill remorse
And black despair, yet a strange silent force
Within her heart, that drew her more and more —
Onward she crawled, and begged from door to door.
Weighed down with weary days, her failing strength
Grew less each hour, till one day's dawn at length,
As its first rays flooded the world with light,
Showed the broad waters, glittering blue and bright,
And where, amid the leafy hawthorn wood,
Just as of old the low white convent stood.
Would any know her? Nay, no fear. Her face
Had lost all trace of youth, of joy, of grace,
Of the pure happy soul they used to know —
The novice Angela — so long ago.
She rang the convent bell. The well-known sound
Smote on her heart, and bowed her to the ground.
And she, who had not wept for long dry years,
Felt the strange rush of unaccustomed tears;
Terror and anguish seemed to check her breath,
And stop her heart — O God! could this be death?
Crouching against the iron gate, she laid
Her weary head against the bars, and prayed:

But nearer footsteps drew, then seemed to wait;
And then she heard the opening of the grate,
And saw the withered face, on which awoke
Pity and sorrow, as the portress spoke,
And asked the stranger's bidding: "Take me in,"
She faltered, "Sister Monica, from sin,
And sorrow, and despair, that will not cease;
Oh take me in, and let me die in peace!"
With soothing words the sister bade her wait,
Until she brought the key to unbar the gate.
The beggar tried to thank her as she lay,
And heard the echoing footsteps die away.
But what soft voice was that which sounded near,
And stirred strange trouble in her heart to hear?
She raised her head; she saw — she seemed to know
A face, that came from long, long years ago:
Herself; yet not as when she fled away,
The young and blooming Novice, fair and gay,
But a grave woman, gentle and serene:
The outcast knew it — what she might have been.
But as she gazed and gazed, a radiance bright
Filled all the place with strange and sudden light;
The nun was there no longer, but instead,
A figure with a circle round its head,
A ring of glory; and a face, so meek,
So soft, so tender. . . . Angela strove to speak,
And stretched her hands out, crying, "Mary mild,
Mother of mercy, help me! — help your child!"
And Mary answered, "From thy bitter past,
Welcome, my child! oh, welcome home at last!
I filled thy place. Thy flight is known to none,
For all thy daily duties I have done;
Gathered thy flowers, and prayed, and sang, and slept;
Didst thou not know, poor child, thy place was kept?
Kind hearts are here; yet would the tenderest one
Have limits to its mercy: God has none.
And man's forgiveness may be true and sweet,
But yet he stoops to give it. More complete
Is love that lays forgiveness at thy feet,
And pleads with thee to raise it. Only Heaven
Means crowned, not vanquished, when it says 'Forgiven!' "

Back hurried Sister Monica; but where
Was the poor beggar she left lying there?
Gone; and she searched in vain, and sought the place
For that wan woman, with the piteous face:
But only Angela at the gateway stood,
Laden with hawthorn blossoms from the wood.

And never did a day pass by again,
But the old portress, with a sigh of pain,
Would sorrow for her loitering: with a prayer
That the poor beggar, in her wild despair,
Might not have come to any ill; and when
She ended, "God forgive her!" humbly then
Did Angela bow her head, and say "Amen!"
How pitiful her heart was! all could trace
Something that dimmed the brightness of her face
After that day, which none had seen before;
Not trouble — but a shadow — nothing more.

Years passed away. Then, one dark day of dread,
Saw all the sisters kneeling round a bed,
Where Angela lay dying; every breath
Struggling beneath the heavy hand of death.
But suddenly a flush lit up her cheek,
She raised her wan right hand, and strove to speak.
In sorrowing love they listened; not a sound
Or sigh disturbed the utter silence round;
The very taper's flames were scarcely stirred,
In such hushed awe the sisters knelt and heard.
And thro' that silence Angela told her life:
Her sin, her flight; the sorrow and the strife,
And the return; and then, clear, low, and calm,
"Praise God for me, my sisters;" and the psalm
Rang up to heaven, far, and clear, and wide,
Again and yet again, then sank and died;
While her white face had such a smile of peace,
They saw she never heard the music cease;
And weeping sisters laid her in her tomb,
Crowned with a wreath of perfumed hawthorn bloom.

And thus the legend ended. It may be
Something is hidden in the mystery,
Besides the lesson of God's pardon, shown
Never enough believed, or asked, or known.
Have we not all, amid life's petty strife,
Some pure ideal of a noble life
That once seemed possible? Did we not hear
The flutter of its wings, and feel it near,
And just within our reach? It was. And yet
We lost it in this daily jar and fret,
And now live idle in a vague regret;
But still our place is kept, and it will wait,
Ready for us to fill it, soon or late.
No star is ever lost we once have seen,
We always may be what we might have been.

Since good, tho' only thought, has life and breath,
God's life can always be redeemed from death;
And evil, in its nature, is decay,
And any hour can blot it all away;
The hopes that, lost, in some far distance seem.
May be the truer life, and this the dream.

Adelaide Anne Proctor – A Short Biography

Adelaide Anne Procter was born on 30th October, 1825 at 25 Bedford Square in the Bloomsbury district of London, to the poet Bryan Waller Procter and his wife Anne (née Skepper).

Procter's literary career began early, whilst still a teenager. Many of her poems were published by the great Charles Dickens in his periodicals Household Words and All the Year Round before being later published in book form.

Indeed, Dickens was formative in her career and spoke highly of her intelligence. She seemed to be able to fully focus and master without difficulty any subject she wished.

As a young child, she became familiar with several of the problems of Euclid. As she grew she added French, Italian, and German as well as piano-forte and drawing to her array of talents. But, it seems that as soon as a subject was mastered her interest passed and she was on to another.

A voracious reader, Procter was largely self-taught, though she did study at Queen's College in Harley Street in 1850. Her interest in poetry grew from an early age. Accounts say that she carried with her a tiny album into which her favourite passages were copied for her by her mother before she herself could write. Preferring poetry to dolls and the like was certainly an indication of her future career path.

Procter published her first poem, Ministering Angels, while still a teenager. The poem appeared in Heath's Book of Beauty in 1843.

By 1853 she was submitting pieces to Dickens's Household Words under her pseudonym Mary Berwick, electing that this way her work would be judged for its own worth rather than on the friendship between her father and Dickens. Dickens didn't learn of her true identity for over a year.

Minstering Angels was to be the beginning of a long and mutually beneficial relationship of publishing in Dickens' journals that would eventually reach 73 poems in House words together with a further 7 poems in All the Year Round, most of which were collected and later published into her first two volumes of poetry, both entitled Legends and Lyrics. Her work was also published in Good Words and Cornhill.

Proctor was also the editor of the journal Victoria Regia, which became the showpiece of the Victoria Press, a venture hoping to promote the employment of women in all manner of trades and professions.

In 1851, Procter had converted to Roman Catholicism and become extremely active in several charitable and feminist causes. She was a member of the Langham Place Group, which set out to improve conditions for women, and was friends with many feminists including Bessie Rayner Parkes and Barbara

Leigh Smith. Procter helped found the English Woman's Journal in 1858 and, in 1859, the Society for the Promotion of the Employment of Women, both of which focused on expanding women's economic and employment opportunities. Though on paper Proctor was merely one member among many, fellow-member Jessie Boucherett considered her to be the "animating spirit" of the Society. Her third volume of poetry, A Chaplet of Verses (1861), was published for the benefit of a Catholic Night Refuge for Women and Children that had been founded in 1860 at Providence Row in East London.

Her personal life remains a little unclear. Accounts suggest that in 1858 Procter became engaged, although to whom remains unknown and the marriage never took place.

Other accounts suggest the engagement lasted several years before being broken off by her fiancé. Another goes so far as to suggest that she was a lesbian and in love with Matilda Hays, a fellow member of the Society for the Promotion of the Employment of Women; other critics have called Procter's relationship with Hays "emotionally intense." Procter's first volume of poetry, Legends and Lyrics (1858) was dedicated to Hays and that same year Procter wrote a poem titled "To M.M.H." in which Procter "expresses love for Hays. Matilda Hays herself was a novelist and translator of George Sand and a somewhat controversial figure. She liked to dress in men's clothes and had lived with the sculptor Harriet Hosmer in Rome earlier in the 1850s." The true extent of her relationship cannot be verified and it should always be seen in proportion to her Catholicism.

Procter's health failed in 1862. Dickens and others suggested that this illness was due to her extensive and exhausting schedule of charity work.

An attempt to improve her health by taking a cure at Malvern failed.

Adelaide Anne Proctor died on 3rd February 1864 of tuberculosis. She had been bed-ridden for almost a year. Procter was buried in Kensal Green Cemetery.

Her death was described in the press as a "national calamity". Indeed, Procter was the favourite poet of Queen Victoria. The Victorian poet Coventry Patmore, himself a highly respected poet of the time, called her the most popular poet of the day, after Alfred, Lord Tennyson. Procter's popularity continued after her death; the first volume of Legends and Lyrics went through 19 editions by 1881, and the second volume through 14 editions by the same year.

Many of her poems were made into hymns or otherwise set to music. Among these was "The Lost Chord", which Arthur Sullivan set to music in 1877, was the most commercially successful of the 1870s and 1880s in both Britain and the United States.

However, by the turn of the century her work had fallen from fashion and has never recovered.

Procter's poetry was strongly influenced by her religious beliefs, charity work and her desire for social reform. Homelessness, poverty, and fallen women are frequent themes in her verse.

Three Evenings in the House,' a short story written for A House to Let (1858), one of the collaborative Christmas numbers of the Charles Dickens' journal Household Words.

Legends and Lyrics. First series (1858)

"The Ghost in the Picture Room" written for A Haunted House (1859)

Legends and Lyrics. Second series (1861)

A Chaplet of Verses (1862)

www.ingramcontent.com/pod-product-compliance
Lightning Source LLC
Chambersburg PA
CBHW060135050426
42448CB00010B/2132